THE ALMOSTS

THE ALMOSTS

A STUDY
OF THE FEEBLE-MINDED

BY

HELEN MacMURCHY

KENNIKAT PRESS
Port Washington, N. Y./London

THE ALMOSTS

First published in '1920
Reissued in 1970 by Kennikat Press
Library of Congress Catalog Card No: 77-115325
ISBN 0-8046-1116-5

Manufactured by Taylor Publishing Company   Dallas, Texas

TO THE MEMORY

OF

MY FATHER AND MY MOTHER

PREFACE

Sir William Osler, with characteristic kindness and generosity, wrote an Introduction to *The Almosts* and forwarded the manuscript from Oxford in the spring of 1919.

To the great loss of the reader, the manuscript never arrived. All efforts to find it have been unavailing, and now the master has laid aside his pen. Nevertheless, he, being dead, yet speaketh and his spirit still abides with his pupils.

To all my fellow-servants who are helping the mentally defective, and by helping them trying to serve humanity, this little book is offered in the hope that in their hands it may be used to advance the work of awakening public interest and educating public opinion.

Helen MacMurchy

Toronto, Canada
January 19, 1920

ACKNOWLEDGMENTS

To the Authors and Publishers who have kindly given permission for the use of quotations in "The Almosts" from the copyright works mentioned in the following list, grateful acknowledgments and thanks are offered.

Malcolm, GEORGE MACDONALD: Messrs. Kegan Paul, Trench, Trübner & Co., Ltd.

Sir Gibbie, GEORGE MACDONALD: Dr. Greville Macdonald, A. P. Watt & Son, and Messrs. Hurst & Blackett, Ltd.

The Wrecker, ROBERT LOUIS STEVENSON and LLOYD OSBOURNE: Messrs. Cassell & Co., Ltd., and Messrs. Charles Scribner's Sons.

The Cruise of the Janet Nichol, MRS. R. L. STEVENSON: Messrs. Charles Scribner's Sons.

Mr. Opp, ALICE HEGAN RICE: Messrs. Hodder & Stoughton and The Century Company.

Marm Lisa, KATE DOUGLAS WIGGIN: Messrs. Houghton Mifflin Company.

Vesty of the Basins, SARA P. McL. GREENE: Messrs. Harper & Brothers.

Bram of the Five Corners, ARNOLD MULDER: Messrs. A. C. McClurg & Co.

Heritages of the Lord, from "The Contributors' Club," *Atlantic Monthly*: The Editor of the *Atlantic Monthly*.

And to many friends who have helped me

CONTENTS

I. SHAKESPEARE: BUNYAN: SCOTT . . . 1
The Fool — The Pilgrim's Progress —
Waverley — Ivanhoe — The Heart of
Mid-Lothian

II. THE MENTAL DEFECTIVES OF DICKENS . 31
Little Dorrit — Barnaby Rudge — Nich-
olas Nickleby — Our Mutual Friend —
Dombey and Son — Bleak House

III. BULWER LYTTON: CHARLES READE: VIC-
TOR HUGO: GEORGE MACDONALD:
GEORGE ELIOT: JOSEPH CONRAD:
ROBERT LOUIS STEVENSON. . . . 101
Ernest Maltravers — Alice — Put Your-
self in His Place — Notre Dame de Paris —
Malcolm — Sir Gibbie — Brother Jacob
— The Idiots — Olalla — The Wrecker

IV. NATHANIEL HAWTHORNE: ALICE HEGAN
RICE: KATE DOUGLAS WIGGIN: SARAH
P. McL. GREENE: ARNOLD MULDER:
THE CONTRIBUTORS' CLUB . . . 145
The Marble Faun — Mr. Opp — Marm
Lisa — Vesty of the Basins — Bram of
the Five Corners — Heritages of the Lord

V. THE CASE FOR THE FEEBLE-MINDED . . 169
Give them a Chance — Easy to Make
Happy, Safe, and Useful

THE ALMOSTS

CHAPTER I

SHAKESPEARE, BUNYAN, SCOTT

SOMETIMES the poet sees more than the scientist, even when the scientific man is playing at his own game. The novelist can give a few points to the sociologist, and the dramatist to the settlement worker. Had the voter and the legislator studied with a little more attention the works of William Shakespeare and Walter Scott we might have come sooner to some of the alleged discoveries of the twentieth century.

Take the case of the feeble-minded. They have been drawn from life more than once by the great masters already mentioned, as well as by Charles Dickens, Victor Hugo, Charles Reade, and many other writers, and yet so far at least we do not seem to have taken mentally defective persons in the world as seriously as the great writers who immortalized Wamba, Quasimodo, Barnaby Rudge, Young Sparkler, Mr. Toots, and others, by giving them the entry to that stage which the world may always watch from the windows of the Library.

There can be no doubt that the "fool," who is so often mentioned by earlier writers and attained his greatest vogue in the fifteenth and sixteenth centuries, was in many cases what we now call a high-grade or middle-grade mental defective. By these writers the words "fool" and "clown" are used almost as synonymous, though the fool was often "a mere idiot or natural, and the clown was often a rustic or shrewd domestic."

Fools are mentioned in the Domesday Book; the Duke of Normandy had a fool or court jester, and so of course had many, if not all, British sovereigns at that time, especially those of the Stuart line. Many anecdotes are told of the fools of James I, and also of the two fools of the Court of Charles I, who were named Archie Armstrong and Muckle John.

In the long line of royal fools there seems to have been only one woman, and she remained unknown until Mrs. C. C. Stopes drew attention to her in an interesting article in the "Athenæum" in August, 1905. Jane was her name and she was attached to the royal household of Queen Mary from 1537 to 1558, and attended her mistress in adversity and prosperity, being attached to her household before she became queen. Mrs. Stopes suggests that Queen Mary may have made this appointment from a modest objection to the jests of her father's fools, or more likely that she had extended her kind protection to Jane as a young girl who peculiarly needed her help.

There seems no reason to regard Jane, whose paternal name is unknown, as in any sense mentally defective. Her wit was probably more comforting than caustic, and all we really know about Jane is that Queen Mary dressed her beautifully in crimson satin, gold brocade, linen, white satin, red silk, French gowns, red satin and red petticoats, and varied and magnificent slippers and shoes. She also on New Year's Day gave a New Year's gift to a "woman dwelling at Burye for healing Jane, the Fool, her eye."

Jane had black satin and crimson belts, Dutch gowns and French gowns, twelve pairs of velvet shoes, silk fringe, green silk; and twelve pairs of leather shoes were bought "for the said Jane, our Fool."

In the English drama, both before and after Shakespeare, fools are introduced, the last play in which this was the case being Shadwell's drama, "The Woman Captain," in 1680. Shakespeare followed the traditions of the drama in this respect, and two, at least, of the fools of Shakespeare are among his triumphs — Touchstone in "All's Well that Ends Well" and the Fool in "Lear." Touchstone is probably mentally defective, but it is quite possible that the Fool in "Lear" may have been insane; though certain of his words and actions remind one forcibly of a mentally defective person. His power of affection is remarkable. So it often is in a mental defective.

Lear's Fool is Shakespeare's own creation. He does not exist in the original from which a large part of the material for this play is drawn. And Shakespeare makes him more of a human being than other dramatists have made any of their fools, thus showing himself again greatest of all.

THE PILGRIM'S PROGRESS

Among the great company of people in this matchless allegory is one Mr. Feeble-mind, rescued by Mr. Great-heart from Giant Slay-good, who "was rifling him, with a purpose after that to pick his bones."

It does not appear, however, that Mr. Feeble-mind was at all mentally defective. He was a nephew of Mr. Fearing, who came from the town of Stupidity, and of whom "father Honest" said, "He was a man that had the Root of the matter in him; but he was one of the most troublesome Pilgrims that ever I met with in all my days." Great-heart, who knew Mr. Fearing well, having been his guide "from my Master's house to the gates of the Celestial City," says of him: "Everything frightned him that he heard any-body speak of, that had but the least appearance of opposition in it. . . . He had, I think, a Slough of Despond in his mind."

Mr. Feeble-mind and his father were born in the town of Uncertain, but he had that firm-ness of resolve and continuity of purpose to which mental defectives are strangers. He says: "I would, if I could, though I can but crawl, spend my life in the Pilgrim's Way . . . this I have resolved on, to wit: to *run* when I can, to *go* when I cannot run, and to *creep* when I cannot go . . . my Way is before me, my mind is beyond the River that has no bridge."

He was evidently regarded as an equal and companion by Gaius and by the other pilgrims. That would not have happened if he had been mentally defective.

"Then Gaius took his leave of them all . . . and particularly of Mr. Feeble-mind."

Great-heart says: "You must needs go along with us, we will wait for you."

" Mr. Ready-to-halt came by, . . . and he also was going on Pilgrimage." He hails Mr. Feeble-mind with joy and says: "I shall be glad of thy company."

Mr. Feeble-mind was certainly one of those referred to in the apostolic injunction, "Comfort the feeble-minded." He was infirm and irresolute, undecided and easily depressed, but his judgment was good on the whole, and his reactions normal. The words in which he bids his friends farewell when the summons comes for him to cross the River that has no bridge are sufficient to show that he is not feeble-minded in the modern sense of that word, but only in the sense in which the apostle used it, somewhat equivalent to Bunyan's term

"chicken-hearted," or to the modern colloqui-
alism, "low in his mind." Like his uncle, Mr.
Fearing, he had "a Slough of Despond in his
mind"; but like him, too, he never had any
inclination to go back and was a good pilgrim
to the end.

The Shepherds, however, showed to Chris-
tiana and her daughter-in-law, Mercy, "one
Fool, and one *Want-wit*, washing of an *Ethio-
pian* with intention to make him white but the
more they washed him the blacker he was."
This is much more like the picture of a mental
defective, but we have only this one allusion to
Fool and Want-wit in John Bunyan's great
allegory, so we cannot make a diagnosis.

WAVERLEY

Sir Walter Scott introduces Davie Gellatley
in one of the early chapters of Waverley.
Edward Waverley is approaching the manor-
house of Tully-Veolan when he sees poor Davie
afar off, and is struck even at that distance with
the oddity of his appearance. This impression
deepens as Davie draws near. His gestures, his
gait, and his attire were all alike grotesque.

A better description of a mentally defective

man is scarcely to be found anywhere than this description of Davie Gellatley. "His gait was as singular as his gestures, for at times he hopped with great perseverance on the right foot, then exchanged that supporter to advance in the same manner on the left, and then putting his feet close together, he hopped upon both at once. His attire, also, was antiquated and extravagant. It consisted in a sort of grey jerkin, with scarlet cuffs and slashed sleeves, showing a scarlet lining; the other parts of the dress corresponded in colour, not forgetting a pair of scarlet stockings, and a scarlet bonnet, proudly surmounted with a turkey's feather. Edward, whom he did not seem to observe, now perceived confirmation in his features of what the mien and gestures had already announced. It was apparently neither idiocy nor insanity which gave that wild, unsettled, irregular expression to a face which naturally was rather handsome, but something that resembled a compound of both, where the simplicity of the fool was mixed with the extravagance of a crazed imagination. He sung with great earnestness, and not without some taste, a fragment of an old Scotch ditty."

"He is an innocent, sir," said the butler; "there is one such in almost every town in the country, but ours is brought far ben. He used to work a day's turn weel eneugh; but he helped Miss Rose when she was flemit with the Laird of Killancureit's new English bull, and since that time we ca' him Davie Do-little; indeed we might ca' him David Do-næthing, for since he got that gay clothing, to please his honour and my young mistress (great folks will have their fancies), he has done nothing but dance up and down about the *town*, without doing a single turn, unless trimming the laird's fishing wand or busking his flies, or maybe catching a dish of trouts at an orra-time."

Sir Walter adds the following footnote:

"I am ignorant how long the ancient and established custom of keeping fools has been disused in England. Swift writes an epitaph on the Earl of Suffolk's fool, —

'Whose name was Dickie Pearce.'

In Scotland the custom subsisted till late in the last century. At Glammis Castle is preserved the dress of one of the jesters, very handsome, and ornamented with many bells. It is not above thirty years since such a character stood by the side-board of a nobleman of the first rank in Scotland, and occasionally mixed in the conversation, till he carried the joke rather too far, in making proposals to one of the young ladies of the family, and publishing the banns betwixt her and himself in the public church."

Davie appears but little in the course of the story until, the ill-fated rebellion over, Edward revisits the ruins of the manor-house, and recognizes Davie's voice again singing an old Scots song. On calling him by name, the poor fellow appears, then hides in terror until Waverley, by whistling a favorite air, induces him to reappear.

"The poor fool himself appeared the ghost of what he had been. The peculiar dress in which he had been attired in better days, showed only miserable rags of its whimsical finery, the lack of which was oddly supplied by the remnants of tapestried hangings, window-curtains, and shreds of pictures, with which he had bedizened his tatters. His face, too, had lost its vacant and careless air, and the poor creature looked hollow-eyed, meagre, half-starved, and nervous to a pitiable degree. —

After long hesitation, he at length approached Waverley with some confidence, stared him sadly in the face, and said, 'A' dead and gane — a' dead and gane!'"

Recognizing Edward as a true friend, Davie guides him to the Baron's hiding-place. On this occasion, Davie's old mother has an opportunity to say a good word for her son, telling Edward that she supposes he never knew that all the eggs which were so well roasted at the Hall-House were "turned by our Davie" — "there's no the like of him anywhere for roasting eggs."

Davie appears for the last time in this great tale after the wedding of Edward and Rose, when he comes up the avenue with the dogs to meet the bridal party, "every now and then stopping to admire the new suit which graced his person, in the same colours as formerly, but bedizened fine enough to have served Touchstone himself. He danced up with his usual ungainly frolics, first to the Baron, and then to Rose, passing his hands over his clothes, crying, 'Bra', Bra', Davie,' and scarce able to sing a bar to an end of his thousand-and-one-songs, for the breathless extravagance of his joy."

There are many things about Davie which
recall mental defectives we have all known.
His gait, his gestures, his fondness for clothes
and notice from others, the fact that he was
clever at something — "there's no the like of
him anywhere for roasting eggs" — his mingled responsibility and irresponsibility, his
childlike happiness, and his fondness for music,
in which he has some little skill. The last trait
is an important one in very many mental defectives and should never be lost sight of in
their training.

IVANHOE

Sir Walter Scott had a keen but kindly eye
for the mental defective. Wamba is one of the
masterpieces in the portrait gallery of the
feeble-minded. He appears in the first chapter
of "Ivanhoe." We may conjecture, perhaps
not altogether correctly, that Wamba was not
responsible for his foolish attire, but the description of his expression and of his general
appearance we recognize at once as giving all
the essential points in the impression which a
feeble-minded person makes upon us.

"The looks of Wamba, on the other hand,

indicated, as usual with his class, a sort of vacant curiosity, and fidgetty impatience of any posture of repose, together with the utmost self-satisfaction respecting his own situation, and the appearance which he made."

Very characteristic — especially the self-satisfaction. Afforded the shelter of his master's roof and supported by his master, as far as food and clothing are concerned, and provided with something else quite as dear to a certain type of mental defective, namely, the opportunity to attract attention — Wamba was the domestic clown of Cedric of Rotherwood. Some clowns may have been the victims of mental disease, some normal, but playing the clown's part, though probably the majority were really high-grade mental defectives. The attention of Wamba, for example, in this opening chapter, could not be secured for more than a few moments at a time, even when danger threatened them, and in the second chapter it is plainly stated that he "could not be prevented from lingering occasionally on the road."

Those who have worked with the feeble-minded and learned by personal experience how much their charges need constant supervision and yet are not always willing to be directed by those whose powers of concentration and intelligence exceed their own, will sympathize with Gurth, whose efforts to keep out of the way of the approaching cavalcade were frustrated by the foolishness of Wamba, as anxious to be in the midst of events as any "little tiny boy" — not old enough to know any better or understand the danger.

Wamba's conversation with the Abbot and the false directions which he gives may easily be paralleled in the present day. The feeble-minded have often a perverse desire to make trouble and are seldom known to give correct information as to roads and houses. They will describe houses and people as being in most fantastic and impossible places. A feeble-minded girl recently pointed a stranger directly to a wood and a field by Lake Ontario, insisting that her mother was to be found in a house south of the wood. She had lived near there for years and must have known that there was neither a house nor a person to be found in that direction.

Not a whit abashed by having been found guilty, in the presence of his master Cedric and all his guests, of having attempted to mislead the Abbot and the Templar, Wamba next distinguishes himself by acting as judge of the Templar's attitude to the Jew — "By my faith," says he, "it would seem the Templars love the Jews' inheritance better than they do their company." The wit evident in this and many other remarks from Wamba with which Scott enlivens the pages of "Ivanhoe" furnish further evidence that the novelist had a wonderfully accurate knowledge of the class whom Wamba represents. Their replies frequently partake of the nature of repartee.

For example, among the inmates of an institution in Ontario are about thirty feeble-minded women. In this little world of their own each has her own place and personal ascendancy. "You are eating too much," said one to another. "That does not make any difference to you, does it?" responded the rebuked one. "You are not paying for it!"

This partial insight into the meaning of things extends even into their own situation and their own mental infirmities. One of the same group of girls was found on a certain morning madly rushing up and down the hall.

On being asked what was the matter with her she said, "I've lost my pail and my scrubbing brush and my soap — I need more brains, that is what is the matter with me, but then what is the use of my wishing I had more brains when I don't make any better use of the brains I have."

A boy who was a very high-grade mental defective, and who was almost but not altogether able to earn his own living when he grew up, seemed to succeed pretty well at school until the class reached the multiplication table. All one winter, night after night, his mother tried to teach him his "tables." Finally the boy said to her, "It is no use, mother, I think the arithmetic corner of my brain was never finished." Could any one have expressed it better?

Wamba, on the contrary, says little or nothing about himself, except on the one occasion referred to below. He does, however, possess some insight into the minds and lives of others, as witness his remark about the feelings of the Lady Rowena towards Maurice De Bracy, when the latter kneels before her with the words, "Conquest, lady, should soften the heart. Let me but know that the Lady Rowena forgives the violence occasioned by an ill-fated passion, and she shall soon learn that De Bracy knows how to serve her in nobler ways."

"I forgive you, Sir Knight," said Rowena, "as a Christian."

"That means," said Wamba, "that she does not forgive him at all."

A still more striking instance is found in the remark of Wamba when he found himself free after Cedric, Athelstane, Lady Rowena, the Jew, and his daughter had all fallen an easy prey to Front-de-Bœuf and his cruel allies —
"I have heard men talk of the blessings of freedom," said Wamba, "but I wish any wise man would teach me what use to make of it now that I have it."

The eugenist and others who study heredity may be interested in the reply of Wamba to Prince John at the Tournament. "Who and what art thou, noble champion?" said Prince John, still laughing.

"A fool by right of descent," answered the Jester. "I am Wamba the Son of Witless, who was the son of Weatherbrain, who was the son of an alderman."

Mischief-makers as the feeble-minded often are, it is somewhat characteristic of them to make good-natured remarks, tending to soothe the anger and rage of those with whom they are. Wamba frequently shows himself in this character, and indeed Sir Walter remarks in chapter xviii that he "was frequently wont to act as peacemaker in the family." He tries to persuade Gurth that Cedric did not really mean to kill his dog, Fangs. "To my thinking now," says Wamba, "our Master did not propose to hurt Fangs, but only to affright him." The same quality is shown again in his request to Cedric a little later to forgive Gurth.

But in both of these last-mentioned incidents we have anticipated the course of the story. Wamba's greatest distinction in the narrative comes in connection with the part he plays in the rescue of Cedric from the castle and again when he is the companion of King Richard the Lion-Hearted himself. In the former it will be remembered that the jester, disguised as a priest, is sent into the castle of Front-de-Bœuf where Cedric is imprisoned. Here we

have once more a true touch from the master
hand of Scott. It is exactly what happens every
day to the feeble-minded. People can persuade
them to do anything. They are very open to
suggestion, and it is not always something
noble that is proposed to them by their moni-
tors, but far more frequently a petty crime,
such as pilfering, or more serious offenses,
such as starting incendiary fires of barns or
houses or placing obstructions on railway lines
which may cause accidents involving a loss
of many lives. Wamba, true to his character,
follows the line of conduct which he sees his
three allies wish him to take, and it is in connection with this that we learn something of his
history. It must here be remarked, however,
that in reference to his allies at this time
Wamba confides to Gurth his plain opinion of
them all, great and small. They are, of course,
the Black Knight, who is finally discovered to
be King Richard himself, Friar Tuck and
Locksley, *alias* Robin Hood. Here is Wamba's summing-up of them, "I trust the valour
of the knight will be truer metal than the
religion of the hermit or the honesty of the
yeoman; for this Locksley looks like a born

deer-stealer and the priest like a lusty hypo-
crite."

This is another example of the knowledge
and insight of the creator of Locksley and of
the host of other characters who people the
world of the Waverley Novels. The feeble-
minded often have the same instinctive knowledge of character that children have. Near the
old Gordon farm at Bayside, on Lake Ontario,
there lived all his life a man who was cared for
and looked after like a child by the farmer and
his family. He was a good worker, as almost all
the feeble-minded who have had good training
are, and every one who came to the house knew
that he was a remarkably accurate judge of
character. It used to be said by the family that
they never made up their minds about any one
who came their way before they had asked this
man what he thought of the newcomer, and
that they had never known his opinion to be
wrong.

To return to "Ivanhoe." It will be remembered that the letter sent by Front-de-Bœuf
and his friends to the besiegers of the castle
required them to send a priest to reconcile

Cedric and Athelstane to God, as they were to be executed before noon. The hermit absolutely declined this opportunity and the rest looked one at another, but Wamba, seeing very well what the others wished, remarked that he "was bred to be a friar, until a brain fever came upon me and left me with just wit enough to be a fool."

How like histories which have been written thousands of times in every large institution for the care of the feeble-minded throughout the land! There has always been some illness or a convulsion, or, most favorite story of all, "A very bright baby before he had a fall, but never the same since." It is very likely that these are in every case correct thus far that the recorded illness or accident did take place, but it was not the real cause of the feeble-mindedness. That lies much farther back.

Once in the presence of Cedric, having gained entrance to the castle in the disguise of a priest, there shines out in Wamba that affection, which is the noblest quality of a human being, and in which the feeble-minded, with the one exception of the moral imbecile, are perhaps not wanting any oftener than their

normal fellows. Poor Wamba has made up his
mind to die in his master's room and stead and
finally persuades Cedric to accept this generous
sacrifice. Nor would he listen to Cedric's plea
that Wamba should die in the stead of Athelstane, saying, "I'll hang for no man but my
own born master." Mental defectives are exceedingly and unselfishly affectionate, with a
touching and childlike submission to and delight in the kindness of those older or wiser
than themselves. They can in almost every
instance be guided by this childlike affection
all through their lives, by those who care for
and understand them, and the exceptions to
this rule are usually mental defectives who
have been neglected and allowed to become
criminal or immoral in habit and life. Once a
taste has been acquired for evil things, it is not
easily lost. But if the mentally defective are
cared for and sheltered from childhood up,
their tastes remain the simple and innocent
tastes of childhood.

To return again to the story. Cedric dons the
priest's vestments and escapes first, but in the
successful assault which takes place immediately, Wamba is also rescued and comes to

great honor as the escort of the disguised king. The last description of him is given at the time when he accompanies the king as his guide. This is again a perfectly correct study of a certain type of the feeble-minded.

"Indeed, the infirmity of Wamba's brain consisted chiefly in a kind of impatient irritability, which suffered him not long to remain quiet in any posture, or to adhere to any certain train of ideas, although he was for a few minutes alert enough in performing any immediate task, or in apprehending any immediate topic. On horseback, therefore, he was perpetually swinging himself backwards and forwards, now on the horse's ears, then anon on the very rump of the animal, now hanging both his legs on one side, and now sitting with his face to the tail, moping, mowing, and making a thousand apish gestures, until his palfrey took his freaks so much to heart, as fairly to lay him at his length on the green grass — an incident which greatly amused the knight, but compelled his companion to ride more steadily thereafter."

Wamba helps to secure the safety of the king, and finally appears "decorated with a new cap and a most gorgeous set of silver bells" at the

wedding of Ivanhoe and the Lady Rowena.
The last words addressed to him in the story
are those pronounced by King Richard —
"Thy good service shall not be forgotten."
We may well take them to heart, for it is in the
power of the feeble-minded to do us and themselves good service if we undertake their care
and training in childhood, and continue it all
through their lives.

The Heart of Mid-Lothian

The readers of Sir Walter Scott's novels will
not fail to remember the Laird of Dumbiedikes, whose death occurs in the early part of
the story. His son and heir, afterwards Laird,
is described on that occasion as a dull, silly
boy of fourteen or fifteen. He is as nearly as
possible a "border-line case."

When David Deans left Woodend, the new
Laird was hardly able to understand the
announcement; although he had seen the furniture moved the day before, he presented himself the following day "before the closed door
of the cottage at Woodend, and seemed as
much astonished at finding it shut against his
approach as if it was not exactly what he had to

expect. On this occasion he was heard to ejacu-
late 'Gude guide us,' which, by those who knew
him, was considered as a very unusual mark
of emotion. From that moment forward Dumbiedikes became an altered man, and the regu-
larity of his movements, hitherto so exemplary,
was as totally disconcerted as those of a boy's
watch when he has broken the main-spring.
Like the index of the said watch did Dumbiedikes spin round the whole bounds of his little
property, which may be likened unto the dial
of the timepiece, with unwonted velocity.
There was not a cottage into which he did not
enter, nor scarce a maiden on whom he did not
stare. But so it was, that although there were
better farmhouses on the land than Woodend,
and certainly much prettier girls than Jeanie
Deans, yet it did somehow befall that the blank
in the Laird's time was not so pleasantly filled
up as it had been. There was no seat accommo-
dated him so well as the 'bunker' at Woodend,
and no face he loved so much to gaze on as
Jeanie Deans's. So, after spinning round and
round his little orbit, and then remaining sta-
tionary for a week, it seems to have occurred
to him that he was not pinned down to circu-

late on a pivot, like the hands of the watch, but possessed the power of shifting his central point, and extending his circle if he thought proper. To realize which privilege of change of place, he bought a pony from a Highland drover, and with its assistance and company stepped, or rather stumbled, as far as Saint Leonard's Crags.

"The Laird's diurnal visits were disagreeable to Jeanie from apprehension of future consequences, and it served much to console her, upon removing from the spot where she was bred and born, that she had seen the last of Dumbiedikes, his laced hat, and tobacco-pipe. The poor girl no more expected he could muster courage to follow her to Saint Leonard's Crags than that any of her apple trees or cabbages which she had left rooted in the 'yard' at Woodend would spontaneously, and unaided, have undertaken the same journey. It was therefore with much more surprise than pleasure, that, on the sixth day after their removal to Saint Leonard's, she beheld Dumbiedikes arrive, laced hat, tobacco-pipe, and all, and, with the self-same greeting of 'How's all wi' ye, Jeanie? — Where's the gudeman?' assume

as nearly as he could the same position in the
cottage at Saint Leonard's which he had so long
and so regularly occupied at Woodend. He was
no sooner, however, seated, than with an unusual exertion of his powers of conversation,
he added, 'Jeanie — I say, Jeanie, woman,'
here he extended his hand towards her shoulder with all the fingers spread out as if to
clutch it, but in so bashful and awkward a
manner, that when she whisked herself beyond its reach, the paw remained suspended
in the air with the palm open, like the claw of
a heraldic griffin — 'Jeanie,' continued the
swain in this moment of inspiration — 'I say,
Jeanie, it's a braw day outby, and the roads
are no that ill for boot-hose."

If this is not mental defect, it is pretty close
to it!

When the tragedy falls upon the family,
"even Dumbiedikes was moved from his
wonted apathy, and, groping for his purse as
he spoke, ejaculated, 'Jeanie, woman! —
Jeanie woman! dinna greet — it's sad wark,
but siller will help it'; and he drew out his
purse as he spoke."

This is not the only occasion when the Laird

offered money. On one occasion he even mentioned thirty pounds. He was, however, unable to manage his horse, when anxious to follow Jeanie on her journey. "I wad gang too," said the landed proprietor, in an anxious, jealous, and repining tone, "but my powny winna for the life o' me gang ony other road than just frae Dumbiedikes to this house-end, and sae straight back again."

When Jeanie Deans finds it necessary to avail herself of the offer of the Laird to lend her money, she is not well treated by Mrs. Balchristie. For once the Laird finds his tongue, and makes short work of putting his housekeeper in her place. When Jeanie tells of walking twenty miles, he is quite upset, and still more so when she tells of London and the queen. "Lunnon — and the queen — and her sister's life!" said Dumbiedikes, whistling for very amazement — "the lassie's demented."

The Laird opens his leathern money bags — "This is my bank, Jeanie lass," he said, looking first at her and then at the treasure, with an air of great complacency, — "nane o' your gold-smith's bills for me — they bring folk to ruin."

Then, suddenly changing the tone, he resolutely said — "Jeanie, I will make you Lady Dumbiedikes afore the sun sets, and ye may ride to Lunnon in your ain coach, if you like."

"Na, Laird," said Jeanie, "that can never be — my father's grief — my sister's situation — the discredit to you."

"That's my business," said Dumbiedikes; "ye wad say naething about that if you werena a fule — and yet I like ye the better for 't — ae wise body's enough in the married state. But if your heart's ower fu', take what silver will serve ye, and let it be when ye come back again — as gude syne as sune."

"But, Laird," said Jeanie, who felt the necessity of being explicit with so extraordinary a lover, "I like another man better than you, and I canna marry ye."

"Another man better than me, Jeanie!" said Dumbiedikes — "how is that possible? It's no possible, woman, ye hae ken'd me sae lang."

Perhaps the Laird thus vindicated himself, and shows himself to be, after all, on the right side of the border-line. At all events he helped

Jeanie to make the journey which saved her sister's life and gave her the means of personal intercession with the queen herself, as told in that scene which is one of the most beautiful passages in the writings of Sir Walter Scott.

CHAPTER II

THERE are many of the works of Charles Dickens which contain sketches of feeble-minded persons — "Little Dorrit," "Barnaby Rudge," "Nicholas Nickleby," "Our Mutual Friend," "Dombey and Son," "Bleak House," and others. In none of these are these sketches more true to life than in "Little Dorrit."

LITTLE DORRIT

Maggy appears before Little Dorrit and Arthur Clennam, when they are taking almost their first walk together, as a strange figure excitedly calling Little Dorrit "Little Mother," and falling down, scattering into the mud the contents of a large basket of potatoes. Little Dorrit speaks softly to the poor child, saying, "What a clumsy child you are," and everybody then helps to pick up the potatoes, Maggy picking up a very few potatoes and a large quantity of mud and smearing her face with her muddy shawl.

There are few descriptions of a mental defective in literature more accurate in every respect than this one.

"She was about eight and twenty, with large bones, large features, large feet and hands, large eyes and no hair. Her large eyes were limpid and almost colourless; they seemed to be very little affected by light, and to stand unnaturally still. There was also that attentive listening expression in her face, which is seen in the faces of the blind; but she was not blind, having one tolerably serviceable eye. Her face was not exceedingly ugly, though it was only redeemed from being so by a smile; a good-humoured smile and pleasant in itself, but rendered pitiable by being constantly there. A great white cap, with a quantity of opaque frilling that was always flapping about, apologized for Maggy's baldness, and made it so very difficult for her old black bonnet to retain its place upon her head, that it held on round her neck like a gypsy's baby. A commission of haberdashers alone could have reported what the rest of her poor dress was made of; but it had a strong general resemblance to sea-weed, with here and there a gigantic tea-leaf. Her shawl looked particularly like a tea-leaf, after long infusion."

Little Dorrit tells Arthur that Maggy is the granddaughter of her own old nurse, and then says, "Maggy, how old are you?" "Ten, mother," said Maggy. And then Little Dorrit with infinite tenderness adds, "You can't think how good she is, or how clever. . . . She goes on errands as well as any one, and is as trustworthy as the Bank of England. She earns her own living entirely."

Arthur asks what Maggy's history is, and Maggy replies, "Little Mother." When asked to tell about her grandmother, Maggy shook her head, made a drinking-vessel of her clenched left hand, drank out of it and said, "Gin." Then beat an imaginary child and said, "Broom-handles and pokers."

"When Maggy was ten years old," said Little Dorrit, watching her face while she spoke, "she had a bad fever, sir, and she has never grown any older ever since."

Little Dorrit then explained that Maggy "was never to be more than ten years old however long she lived."

This is an interesting forecast or prophecy of

the "mental age" that we now hear so much of. After all, novelists and poets are the best teachers, and experts would do well to learn from them.

Finally Little Dorrit states that, "At length, in course of time, Maggy began to take pains to improve herself, and to be very attentive and very industrious; and by degrees was allowed to come in and out as often as she liked, and got enough to do to support herself. 'And that,' said Little Dorrit, clapping the two great hands together again, 'is Maggy's history as Maggy knows!'

"Ah! But Arthur would have known what was wanting to its completeness, though he had never heard the words 'Little Mother'; though he had never seen the fondling of the small spare hand; though he had had no sight for the tears now standing in the colourless eyes; though he had had no hearing for the sob that checked the clumsy laugh. The dirty gateway with the wind and rain whistling through it, and the basket of muddy potatoes waiting to be spilt again or taken up, never seemed the common hole it really was, when he looked back to it by these lights. Never, never!"

All this again is an anticipation by the great writer of the results of modern study and training, down to the very latest plans of those who rightly hold that there are not a few of the feeble-minded who can be trained and supervised so as to make them safe in the community under the supervision of such a person as Little Dorrit, or who can live in an institution and be allowed to go out by the day to work if they are escorted to and fro by some kind and reliable person, thus earning their own living more or less.

Another character in "Little Dorrit" of supreme interest to us in the study of mental defectives is the great Mrs. Merdle's son, Young Sparkler, who first appears in the story by proxy, as it were, in a conversation between the delightful Fanny and Mrs. Merdle, at which Little Dorrit is present. Fanny requests Mrs. Merdle to let her sister know, "that I had already had the honour of telling your son that I wished to have nothing whatever to say to him." And when the interview is over and Mrs. Merdle has mentioned that she had taken a bracelet from her arm and clasped it on Fanny's, and that Fanny "was so obliging as to allow me to present her with a mark or two of my appreciation at my dressmaker's, and when the sisters came downstairs with powder before and powder behind and were shut out into unpowdered Harley Street, Cavendish Square, Little Dorrit stammered out, 'You did not like this young man, Fanny!' 'Like him,' said Fanny, 'he is almost an idiot.'"

Thus accurately does the fair Fanny make a diagnosis of the modern moron.

Edmund Sparkler himself scarcely appears in person before chapter xxxiii, and his inane conversation about a girl with no nonsense about her confirms Fanny's opinion.

In Book II, when riches have overtaken the Dorrits and opened the prison doors for them, the *entourage* of Mrs. Merdle and her distinguished son Mr. Edmund Sparkler collides with the Dorrit *entourage* over the right to a suite of rooms somewhere in Italy, and Young Sparkler protests to Edward Dorrit, Esquire, "Let you and I try to make this all right. Lady so very much wishes no Row."

At this moment Edmund catches sight of

Miss Fanny herself and stands rooted to the ground, even the maternal command failing to put him in motion, so fixed were his feet.

However agreeable this encounter was to Miss Fanny and however much it gave her to think of, there are few who will read this passage without remembering types of mental defectives very much like Young Sparkler. This is not the voluble type of moron. One of the most interesting things about this type is the superhuman efforts made by them to think and talk as shown above, and again in conversation, for example, with Mr. Dorrit, when the former inquired what Mr. Henry Gowan painted, "Mr. Sparkler opined that he painted anything if he could get the job."

Miss Fanny, like other ladies known to novelists, had ideas of her own, and one evening remarked to her sister, "Amy, I am going to put something into your little head! . . . And remember my words. Mrs. General has designs on Pa." Overruling all Amy's scruples we come in the conversation to the following masterpiece:

"At least, you may be mistaken, Fanny. Now, may you not?"

"Oh, yes, I *may* be," said Fanny, "but I am not. However, I am glad you can contemplate such an escape, my dear, and I am glad that you can take this for the present with sufficient coolness to think of such a chance. It makes me hope that you may be able to bear. . . . I should not try. I'd marry Young Sparkler first."

"Oh, you would never marry him, Fanny, under any circumstances."

"Upon my word, my dear," rejoined that young lady, with exceeding indifference, "I would n't positively answer even for that. There's no knowing what might happen. Especially as I would have many opportunities, afterwards, of treating that woman, his mother, in her own style. Which I most decidedly should not be slow to avail myself of, Amy."

Mr. Sparkler was so fortunate as to persuade Fanny to take care of him, even though Amy went so far as to say, "Dear Fanny, let me say first, that I would far rather we worked for a scanty living again, than I would see you rich and married to Mr. Sparkler."

"Thenceforward, Amy observed Mr. Spark-

ler's treatment by his enslaver, with new reasons for attaching importance to all that
passed between them. There were times when
Fanny appeared quite unable to endure his
mental feebleness, and when she became so
sharply impatient of it that she would all but
dismiss him for good. There were other times
when she got on much better with him; when
he amused her and when her sense of superior-
ity seemed to counterbalance that opposite
side of the scale. If Mr. Sparkler had been
other than the faithfullest and most submissive
of swains, he was sufficiently hard-pressed to
have fled from the scene of his trials, and to
have set at least the whole distance from Rome
to London between himself and his enchan-
tress. But he had no greater will of his own
than a boat has when it is towed by a steamship; and he followed his cruel mistress through
rough and smooth, on equally strong com-
pulsion.

"It might have been a month or six weeks
after the night of the advice, when Little
Dorrit began to think she detected some new
understanding between Mr. Sparkler and
Fanny. Mr. Sparkler, as if in adherence to

some compact, scarcely ever spoke without first looking towards Fanny for leave. That young lady was too discreet ever to look back again; but, if Mr. Sparkler had permission to speak, she remained silent; if he had not, she herself spoke. Moreover, it became plain that whenever Henry Gowan attempted to perform the friendly office of drawing him out, that he was not to be drawn. And not only that, but Fanny would presently, without any pointed application in the world, chance to say something with such a sting in it, that Gowan would draw back as if he had put his hand into a bee-hive."

In one conversation in which Mr. Sparkler endeavors to assert himself he assures Amy five times that "There is no nonsense about Fanny!"

One rather thinks that more than one of the Merdle family and one of the Dorrit family, namely, Edward Dorrit, Esquire, are, to say the least, border-line cases. Perhaps, however, any deficiencies on their part are made up by the penetration of Miss Fanny which sometimes approaches the uncanny. As everybody knows she amply revenged herself upon the

Bosom by presenting to that estimable lady's-maid before her face "appreciations from her dressmaker" and a bracelet, of at least ten times the value of those presented to Fanny herself in the days of their poverty.

Mr. Sparkler makes his last appearance in a conversation with his wife, when, though he does his best, he does not succeed as well as one would like in pleasing that lady, partly because his parrot phrase about "A remarkably fine woman with no nonsense about her" is repeated so often that the fair Fanny can bear it no more.

Barnaby Rudge

The most famous of all Dickens's feeble-minded people is Barnaby Rudge. Barnaby, around whom the story may be said in a sense to center, was, as every reader of Dickens knows, the idiot son of a poor widow whose husband was supposed to have been murdered, along with his master, under peculiarly distressing and brutal circumstances. It was Rudge himself who was the murderer, and who had escaped by dressing himself in the clothes of the servant who had been the other victim.

It was, of course, the reappearance of this terrible man and of Dickens's worst villain, Stagg, that drove the poor widow distracted from time to time and was the reason of her many and painful wanderings.

The description of the poor idiot boy is true to life, but the impression left upon the mind of the reader that the boy's mental defect was caused by the terrible circumstances already alluded to, which occurred immediately before his birth, is not at all likely to be correct, as we now know.

When the honest locksmith, Gabriel Varden, finds the unconscious body of Edward Chester, Barnaby is represented as waving a torch and dancing around the apparently lifeless body.

"As he stood at that moment, half shrinking back and half bending forward, both his face and figure were full in the strong glare of the link, and as distinctly revealed as though it had been broad day. He was about three and twenty years old, and, though rather spare, of a fair height and strong make. His hair, of which he had a great profusion, was red, and, hanging in disorder about his face and shoulders, gave to his restless looks an expression quite unearthly — enhanced by the paleness of his complexion, and the glassy lustre of his large, protruding eyes. Startling as his aspect was, the features were good, and there was something even plaintive in his wan and haggard aspect. But the absence of the soul is far more terrible in a living man than in a dead one, and in this unfortunate being its noblest powers were wanting.

"His dress was of green clumsily trimmed here and there — apparently by his own hands — with gaudy lace; brightest where the cloth was most worn and soiled, and poorest where it was at the best. A pair of tawdry ruffles dangled at his wrists, while his throat was nearly bare. He had ornamented his hat with a cluster of peacock's feathers, but they were limp, and broken, and now trailed negligently down his back. Girt to his side was the steel hilt of an old sword without blade or scabbard; and some parti-coloured ends of ribands and poor glass toys completed the ornamental portion of his attire. The fluttered and confused disposition of all the motley scraps that formed his dress bespoke, in a scarcely less degree than his eager and unsettled manner, the disorder of his mind, and by a grotesque contrast set off and heightened the more impressive wildness of his face."

Those who are familiar with the appearance of mental defectives and their fondness for bright colors will recognize this description.

The restlessness of Barnaby, so characteristic of mental defect, is referred to by his mother, and the remarks that kind people will often make about fancied improvement are well illustrated in the locksmith's words, "In good time," said he in answer to the widow's wish for improvement, "In good time — don't be downhearted. He grows wiser every day." It is no kindness to tell the poor parents that their child will "grow out of" mental defect. Never. Never. Never.

Barnaby and his raven dominate the story. The raven is his great companion, and Barnaby's description of him and his own shadow shows that he apparently has some conception of his own mental condition. This sometimes, but not often, occurs in the feeble-minded.

"He's a merry fellow, that shadow, and keeps close to me, though I *am* silly. We have such

pranks, such walks, such runs, such gambols
on the grass! Sometimes he'll be half as tall as
a church steeple, and sometimes no bigger than
a dwarf. Now, he goes on before, and now behind, and anon he'll be stealing slyly on, on
this side or on that, stopping whenever I stop,
and thinking I can't see him, though I have my
eye on him sharp enough. Oh! he's a merry
fellow. Tell me — is he silly too! I think he is."

Barnaby and his skein of string illustrate
the occupations habitual to some feeble-minded
persons.

Barnaby's journeys are also typical of the
uncared-for and untrained feeble-minded who
often have a great instinct for wandering and
cause no little trouble by their doings at such
times.

It is evident that Barnaby was at least not
idiotic, but of a higher grade, probably an imbecile, when we consider his doings in the
political troubles which form the center of interest in the latter part of this book.

The widow's prayer for her poor son is very
touching: "O Thou," she cried, "who hast
taught me such deep love for this one remnant
of the promise of a happy life, out of whose

affliction, even, perhaps the comfort springs that he is ever a relying, loving child to me — never growing old or cold at heart but needing my care and duty in his manly strength as in his cradle-time — help him in his darkened walk through this sad world, or he is doomed and my poor heart is broken."

Nor was Barnaby without joy and happiness along his darkened path. For example, when his poor mother was driven out of the humble cottage that had been their refuge —

"The widow, to whom each painful mile seemed longer than the last, toiled wearily along; while Barnaby, yielding to every inconstant impulse, fluttered here and there, now leaving her far behind, now lingering far behind himself, now darting into some by-lane or path and leaving her to pursue her way alone, until he stealthily emerged again and came upon her with a wild shout of merriment, as his wayward and capricious nature prompted. Now he would call to her from the topmost branch of some high tree by the roadside; now, using his tall staff as a leaping-pole, come flying over ditch or hedge or five-barred gate; now run with surprising swiftness for a mile or more on

the straight road, and halting, sport upon a
patch of grass with Grip till she came up.
These were his delights; and when his patient
mother heard his merry voice, or looked into
his flushed and healthy face, she would not
have abated them by one sad word or murmur,
though each had been to her a source of suffering in the same degree that it was to him a
pleasure.

"It is something to look upon enjoyment, so
that it be free and wild and in the face of nature, though it is but the enjoyment of an
idiot. It is something to know that Heaven has
left the capacity of gladness in such a creature's breast; it is something to be assured that,
however lightly men may crush that faculty
in their fellows, the Great Creator of mankind
imparts it even to his despised and slighted
work. Who would not rather see a poor idiot
happy in the sunlight, than a wise man pining
in a darkened jail!"

Charles Dickens touches here upon one of
the most important principles in guiding the
feeble-minded, and in advising their relatives.
Do we remember how happy we were in childhood? We could not be made unhappy, largely

because we could not understand the griefs
and burdens of our elders. And the feeble-
minded have been well called "permanent
children." We can always make them happy.
They never grow too old for simple childish
enjoyments. They cannot be acquainted with
grief except in a childish way. They can always
make themselves happy if we let them.

Barnaby's occupations and the fact that he
could help to earn his living are well told in the
following:

"For Barnaby himself, the time which had
flown by had passed him like the wind. The
daily suns of years had shed no brighter gleam
of reason on his mind; no dawn had broken on
his long, dark night. He would sit sometimes
— often for days together — on a low seat by
the fire or by the cottage door, busy at work
(for he had learned the art his mother plied,}
and listening, God help him, to the tales she
would repeat as a lure to keep him in her sight.
He had no recollection of these little narra-
tives; the tale of yesterday was new upon the
morrow; but he liked them at the moment;
and, when the humour held him, would remain
patiently within doors, hearing her stories like

a little child, and working cheerfully from sunrise until it was too dark to see.

"At other times — and then their scanty earnings were barely sufficient to furnish them with food, though of the coarsest sort — he would wander abroad from dawn of day until the twilight deepened into night."

To this humble home that the poor widow made, the blind man by some unhappy chance makes his way and states that his name is Stagg and demands that the poor woman shall pay the relatively enormous sum of twenty pounds to him for the benefit of her wretched husband, expecting that she will apply for the sum to Mr. Haredale, who always paid her an annuity while she lived at her old home. The widow gives this blind wretch six guineas, saying, "These have been scraped together and laid by, lest sickness or death should separate my son and me. They have been purchased at the price of much hunger, hard labor, and want of rest. If you *can* take them — do — on condition that you leave this place upon the instant, and enter no more into that room, where he sits now, expecting your return." She arranges with Stagg to come back that day week at sunset for the remainder of the sum, and in the meantime makes her way to London, frightened most of all by the efforts of the blind man to induce her son to leave her and to awaken in his poor mind the lust for gold.

"How often on their journey did the widow remember with a grateful heart that out of his deprivation Barnaby's cheerfulness and affection sprung! How often did she call to mind that but for that he might have been sullen, morose, unkind, far removed from her — vicious, perhaps, and cruel! How often had she cause for comfort, in his strength, and hope, and in his simple nature! Those feeble powers of mind which rendered him so soon forgetful of the past, save in brief gleams and flashes — even they were a comfort now. The world to him was full of happiness; in every tree, and plant, and flower, in every bird, and beast, and tiny insect whom a breath of summer wind laid low upon the ground, he had delight. His delight was hers; and where many a wise son would have made her sorrowful, this poor light-hearted idiot filled her breast with thankfulness and love."

The impression made by the blind man on

Barnaby was not so evanescent and apparently not unfavorable. He remembered about the gold which was to be found where people crowded and not among trees and quiet places. "He is a wise man," said Barnaby, and spoke about the matter more than once with a certain approval. In this the opinion of Dickens hardly agrees with that of many other observers who are wont to notice that mental defectives, like many little children, have an instinctive knowledge of character.

Another instance of the same thing is the story of Barnaby following Gashford and Lord George Gordon, in spite of the remonstrances of his mother —

"No, no, my lord, forgive me," implored the widow, laying both her hands upon his breast, and scarcely knowing what she did or said in the earnestness of her supplication; "but there are reasons why you should hear my earnest mother's prayer, and leave my son to me. Oh, do. He is not in his right senses, he is not, indeed!"

"It is a bad sign of the wickedness of these times," said Lord George, evading her touch, and colouring deeply, "that those who cling to the truth and support the right cause are set down as mad. Have you the heart to say this of your own son, unnatural mother!"

"I am astonished at you!" said Gashford, with a kind of meek severity. "This is a very sad picture of female depravity."

"He has surely no appearànce," said Lord George, glancing at Barnaby, and whispering in his secretary's ear, "of being deranged? And even if he had we must not construe any trifling peculiarity into madness."

Lord George is by no means the only one who has failed to recognize the feeble-minded, and even magistrates have been heard to use the same words as the miserable Gashford, "He is as sensible and self-possessed as any one I ever saw."

So Barnaby goes to destruction — "She was thrown to the ground; the whole field was in motion; Barnaby was whirled away into the heart of a dense mass of men and she saw him no more."

Hugh knows only too well what use can be made of Barnaby —

"I knew I was not mistaken in Barnaby. Don't you see, man," he added in a whisper,

as he slipped to the other side of Dennis, "that
the lad's a natural, and can be got to do anything, if you take him the right way. Letting
alone the fun he is, he's worth a dozen men, in
earnest, as you'd find if you tried a fall with
him. Leave him to me. You shall soon see
whether he's of use or not."

Hugh is not the only person, who, with criminal intent, has tried to make a mental defective party to a crime. Barnaby did not even
know enough to flee with the rest, and placed
himself in the most unhappy position of all the
rioters.

As to the amount of harm that a poor imbecile like Barnaby can do —

"The proclamation having been produced
and read by one of them, the officer called on
Barnaby to surrender. . . . Still he offered no
reply. Indeed, he had enough to do to run his
eye backward and forward along the half-
dozen men who immediately fronted him, and
settle hurriedly within himself which of them
he would strike first, when they pressed on
him. He caught the eye of one in the centre,
and resolved to hew that fellow down, though
he died for it.

"Again there was a dead silence, and again the same voice called upon him to deliver himself up.

"Next moment he was back in the stable, dealing blows about him like a madman. Two of the men lay stretched at his feet; the one he had marked dropped first — he had a thought for that, even in the hot blood and hurry of the struggle. Another blow — another! Down, mastered, wounded in the breast by a heavy blow from the butt end of a gun (he saw the weapon in the act of falling) — breathless — and a prisoner.".

Meeting his father in Newgate Prison, and escaping with him to take refuge "in a corner of the market among the pens for cattle, Barnaby knelt down, and pausing every now and then to pass his hand over his father's face, or look up to him with a smile, knocked off his irons. When he had seen him spring, a free man, to his feet and had given vent to the transport of delight which the sight awakened, he went to work upon his own which soon went rattling to the ground, and left his limbs unfettered."

He then made for the fields and "found in a pasture near Finchley a poor shed, with walls of mud, and roof of grass and brambles, built for some cow-herd but now deserted. Here they lay down for the rest of the night.

"They wandered to and fro when it was day, and once Barnaby went off alone to a cluster of little cottages two or three miles away, to purchase some bread and milk. But finding no better shelter, they returned to the same place, and lay down again to wait for night."

Barnaby then goes off with great delight to find the blind man and encounters Hugh. Angry and afraid of Hugh, his father is displeased with Barnaby for having brought him to their poor refuge.

"I recollect the man," his father murmured. "Why did you bring him here?"

"Because he would have been killed if I had left him over yonder. They were firing guns and shedding blood. Does the sight of blood turn you sick, father? I see it does by your face. That's like me — what are you looking at?"

"At nothing!" said the murderer softly, as he started back a pace or two, and gazed with sunken jaw and staring eyes above his son's head. "At nothing!"

"He remained in the same attitude and with the same expression on his face for a minute or more; then glanced slowly around as if he had lost something; and went shivering back towards the shed —

"Shall I bring him in, father?" said Barnaby, who had looked on, wondering.

"He only answered with a suppressed groan, and, lying down upon the ground, wrapped his cloak about his head, and shrunk into the darkest corner.

"Finding that nothing would rouse Hugh now, or make him sensible for a moment, Barnaby dragged him along the grass, and laid him upon a little heap of refuse hay and straw, which had been his own bed; first having brought some water from a running stream hard by, and washed his wound, and laved his hands and face. Then he lay down himself, between the two, to pass the night, and, looking at the stars fell fast asleep."

At last Barnaby is found by his mother in prison, the place where so many mental defectives are thrown, and she has to tell him about his father.

In the time of great need the kind locksmith,

Gabriel Varden, comes to the rescue of Barnaby and his mother.

"Mary Rudge will have a home and a firm friend when she most wants one; but Barnaby — poor Barnaby — willing Barnaby — what aid can I render him? There are many, many men of sense, God forgive me," cried the honest locksmith, stopping in a narrow court to pass his hand across his eyes, "I could better afford to lose than Barnaby. We have always been good friends, but I never knew till now how much I loved the lad."

"There were not many in the great city who thought of Barnaby that day, otherwise than as an actor in a show which was to take place to-morrow. But, if the whole population had had him in their minds, and had wished his life to be spared, not one among them could have done so with a purer zeal or a greater singleness of heart than the good locksmith.

"They walked out into the courtyard, clinging to each other, but not speaking. Barnaby knew that the jail was a dull, miserable, sad place, and looked forward to to-morrow as to a passage from it to something bright and beautiful. He had a vague impression too that

he was expected to be brave, that he was a man
of great consequence, and that the prison people would be glad to make him weep. He trod
the ground more firmly as he thought of this,
and bade her take heart and cry no more, and
feel how steady his hand was. 'They call me
silly, mother, They shall see — to-morrow!'

"He was the only one of the three who had
washed or trimmed himself that morning.
Neither of the others had done so since their
doom was pronounced. He still wore the broken
peacock's feathers in his hat; and all his usual
scraps of finery were carefully disposed about
his person. His kindling eye, his firm step, his
proud and resolute bearing, might have graced
some lofty act of heroism; some voluntary sacrifice, born of a noble cause and pure enthusiasm, rather than that felon's death."

Barnaby is rescued just in time by the efforts
of Mr. Haredale and Edward Chester.

"Some time elapsed before Barnaby got the
better of the shock he had sustained, or re-
gained his old health and gayety. But he
recovered by degrees; and although he could
never separate his condemnation and escape
from the idea of a terrific dream, he became,

in other respects, more rational. Dating from
the time of his recovery, he had better memory
and greater steadiness of purpose; but a dark
cloud overhung his whole previous existence,
and never cleared away.

"He was not the less happy for this; for his
love of freedom and interest in all that moved
or grew, or had its being in the elements, remained to him unimpaired. He lived with his
mother on the Maypole farm, tending the poul-
try and the cattle, working in a garden of his
own, and helping everywhere. He was known
to every bird and beast about the place, and
had a name for every one. Never was there a
lighter-hearted husbandman, a creature more
popular with young and old, a blither or more
happy soul than Barnaby; and though he was
free to ramble where he would, he never quitted
Her, but was forever more her stay and comfort.

"It was remarkable that although he had
that dim sense of the past, he sought out
Hugh's dog, and took him under his care; and
that he never could be tempted into London.
When the riots were many years old, and
Edward and his wife came back to England

with a family almost as numerous as Dolly's and one day appeared at the Maypole porch, he knew them instantly, and wept and leaped for joy. But neither to visit them, nor on any other pretence, no matter how full of promise and enjoyment, could he be persuaded to set foot in the streets; nor did he ever conquer his repugnance or look upon the town again."

On the whole, the character of Barnaby Rudge, though presenting many interesting features, can hardly be said to be Dickens's greatest success in the portrayal of feeble-minded persons. It is too much influenced by the thought of the time. The author shows himself here rather abreast of the current opinion in his time about mental defectives. But in many of his other feeble-minded characters he shows himself far ahead of such opinion.

NICHOLAS NICKLEBY

In none of Dickens's works is there a more instructive picture of a mentally defective boy than in Nicholas Nickleby.

When Nicholas reaches Dotheboys Hall he observed "that the school was a long, cold-looking house, one story high, with a few straggling out-buildings behind, and a barn and stable adjoining. After the lapse of a minute or two, the noise of somebody unlocking the yard gate was heard, and presently a tall, lean boy, with a lantern in his hand, issued forth.

"Is that you, Smike?" cried Squeers.

"Yes, sir," replied the boy.

"Then why the devil did n't you come before?"

"Please, sir, I fell asleep over the fire," answered Smike, with humility.

"Fire! what fire? Where's there a fire?" demanded the schoolmaster sharply.

"Only in the kitchen, sir," replied the boy. "Missus said as I was sitting up I might go in there for a warm."

"Your Missus is a fool," retorted Squeers. "You'd have been a deuced deal more wakeful in the cold, I'll engage."

When Squeers sorted the mail poor Smike "glanced with an anxious and timid expression at the papers, as if with a sickly hope that one among them might relate to him."

In answer to the poor boy's inquiry, "Have you — did anybody — has nothing been heard — about me?" Squeers replies, "Devil a bit."

"The boy put his hand to his head as if he were making an effort to recollect something, and then, looking vacantly at his questioner, gradually broke into a smile, and limped away.

"I'll tell you what, Squeers," remarked his wife, as the door closed, "I think that young chap's turning silly."

"I hope not," said the schoolmaster, "for he's a handy fellow out of doors, and worth his meat and drink, anyway. I should think he'd have wit enough for us though, if he was."

We are again reminded of the fact so well known to those who have the care of the feeble-minded — they can earn their living in an institution. Even Squeers knew this. The name of the institution in this case was Dotheboys Hall.

The description of the boys of Dotheboys Hall is almost too heartrending to quote, except that it reminds us that we *have* made some progress. Whether there ever was such a school as Dotheboys Hall or not, probably there were places almost as bad, and one can feel that such a place is not possible now.

"Pale and haggard faces, lank and bony figures, children with the countenances of old men, deformities with irons upon their limbs, boys of stunted growth, and others whose long meagre legs would hardly bear their stooping bodies, all crowded on the view together; there were the bleared eye, the hare-lip, the crooked foot, and every ugliness or distortion that told of unnatural aversion conceived by parents for their offspring, or of young lives which, from the earliest dawn of infancy, had been one horrible endurance of cruelty and neglect. There were little faces which should have been handsome, darkened with the scowl of sullen, dogged suffering; there was childhood with the light of its eye quenched, its beauty gone, and its helplessness alone remaining; there were vicious-faced boys, brooding, with leaden eyes, like malefactors in a jail; and there were young creatures on whom the sins of their frail parents had descended, weeping even for the mercenary nurses they had known, and lonesome even in their loneliness. With every kindly sympathy and affection blasted in its birth, with every young and healthy feeling flogged and starved down, with every revengeful passion that can fester in swollen hearts eating its evil way to their core in silence, what an incipient Hell was breeding here!"

Have we abolished all our "unnecessary Hells?" Let us make a clean job of it!

The coming of Nicholas Nickleby was a blessing to poor Smike.

"Smike, since the night Nicholas had spoken kindly to him in the school-room, had followed him to and fro, with an ever restless desire to serve or help him; anticipating such little wants as his humble ability could supply, and content only to be near him. He would sit beside him for hours, looking patiently into his face; and a word would brighten up his careworn visage, and call into it a passing gleam, even of happiness. He was an altered being; he had an object now; and that object was to show his attachment to the only person — that person a stranger — who had treated him, not to say with kindness, but like a human creature.

"Upon this poor being, all the spleen and ill-humour that could not be vented on Nicholas were unceasingly bestowed. Drudgery would have been nothing — Smike was well used to that. Buffetings inflicted without cause, would have been equally a matter of course; for to them, also, he had served a long and weary apprenticeship; but it was no sooner observed that he had become attached to Nicholas, than stripes and blows, stripes and blows, morning, noon, and night, were his only portion. Squeers was jealous of the influence which his man had so soon acquired, and his family hated him, and Smike paid for both. Nicholas saw it and ground his teeth at every repetition of the savage and cowardly attack."

The grave mental defect of the poor boy is thus clearly described:

"Vainly endeavouring to master some task which a child of nine years old, possessed of ordinary powers, could have conquered with ease, but which, to the addled brain of the crushed boy of nineteen, was a sealed and hopeless mystery. Yet there he sat, patiently conning the page again and again, stimulated by no boyish ambition, for he was the common jest and scoff even of the uncouth objects that congregated about him, but inspired by the one eager desire to please his solitary friend."

We should not ask mental defectives to do the impossible. It is cruel.

Nicholas begins to think of leaving the Hall, and says Smike will be better off when he (Nicholas) goes. The scene in which the young master settles accounts once for all with Squeers and his family, and, taking Smike with him, leaves the place forever, has perhaps no rival in Dickens's works, unless it be that scene in which Micawber settles his accounts with Uriah Heep or that in which Miss Betsey Trotwood avenges us all upon Miss Murdstone.

Smike soon begins to feel that he is a burden to his benefactor: "I know you are unhappy, and have got into great trouble by bringing me away. I ought to have known that, and stopped behind — I would, indeed, if I had thought it then. You — you — are not rich; you have not enough for yourself and I should not be here. You grow," said the lad, laying his hand timidly on that of Nicholas, "you grow thinner every day; your cheek is paler and your eye more sunk. Indeed I cannot bear to see you so, and think how I am burdening you. I tried to go away to-day, but the thought of your kind face drew me back. I could not leave you without a word." The poor fellow could say no more, for his eyes filled with tears, and his voice was gone.

"The word which separates us," said Nicholas, grasping him heartily by the shoulder, "shall never be said by me, for you are my only comfort and stay. I would not lose you now, Smike, for all the world could give. The thought of you has upheld me through all I have endured to-day, and shall, through fifty times such trouble. Give me your hand. My heart is linked to yours. We will journey from this place together before the week is out. What if I am steeped in poverty? You lighten it, and we will be poor together."

They set out for Portsmouth, and no sooner does Crummles, the theatrical manager, see Smike than he does what we should all try to do in caring for the mentally defective. He sees what Smike is good for.

"Excuse my saying so," said the manager, leaning over to Nicholas and sinking his voice, "but what a capital countenance your friend has got!"

"Poor fellow!" said Nicholas, with a half smile, "I wish it were a little more plump and less haggard."

"Plump!" exclaimed the manager, quite horrified, "you'd spoil it forever."

"Do you think so?"

"Think so, sir! Why, as he is now," said the manager, striking his knee emphatically; "without a pad upon his body, and hardly a touch of paint upon his face, he'd make such an actor for the starved business as was never seen in this country. Only let him be tolerably well up in the Apothecary in 'Romeo and Juliet,' with the slightest possible dab of red on the tip of his nose, and he'd be certain of three rounds the moment he put his head out of the practicable door in the front grooves O.P."

And Nicholas, sheer destitution staring him in the face, and thinking most of all of his helpless charge, forthwith goes on the stage. His efforts to teach Smike his lines will appeal to those who have been in a like position.

Smike, who had to sustain the character of the Apothecary, had been as yet wholly unable to get any of the part into his head but the general idea that he was very hungry, which — perhaps from old recollections — he had acquired with great aptitude.

"I don't know what's to be done, Smike,"

said Nicholas, laying down the book. "I'm afraid you can't learn it, my poor fellow."

"I am afraid not," said Smike, shaking his head. "I think if you — but that would give you so much trouble."

"What?" inquired Nicholas. "Never mind me."

"I think," said Smike, "if you were to keep saying it to me in little bits, over and over again, I should be able to recollect it from hearing you."

"Do you think so!" exclaimed Nicholas. "Well said. Let us see who tires first. Not I, Smike, trust me. Now then. 'Who calls so loud?'"

"'Who calls so loud?'" said Smike.

"'Who calls so loud?'" repeated Nicholas.

"'Who calls so loud?'" cried Smike.

"Thus they continued to ask each other who called so loud, over and over again; and when Smike had that by heart, Nicholas went to another sentence, and then to two at a time, and then to three, and so on, until at midnight poor Smike found to his unspeakable joy that he really began to remember something about the text.

"Early in the morning they went to it again, and Smike, rendered more confident by the progress he had already made, got on faster and with better heart. As soon as he began to acquire the words pretty freely, Nicholas showed him how he must come in with both hands spread out upon his stomach, and how he must occasionally rub it, in compliance with the established form by which people on the stage always denote that they want something to eat. After the morning's rehearsal they went to work again, nor did they stop, except for a hasty dinner, until it was time to repair to the theatre at night.

"Never had master a more anxious, humble, docile pupil. Never had pupil a more patient, unwearying, considerate, kind-hearted master.

"As soon as they were dressed, and at every interval when he was not upon the stage, Nicholas renewed his instructions. They prospered well. The Romeo was received with hearty plaudits and unbounded favour, and Smike was pronounced unanimously, alike by audience and actors, the very prince and prodigy of Apothecaries."

The license of the story-teller is somewhat in

evidence here. It is not every boy like poor
Smike who could recollect his part. But some
mental defectives could do the part to per-
fection, and evidently Smike was one.

We now find a reference to the most serious
problem in the care of the mental defective at
large in the world. It is a mere hint.

"You are out of spirits," said Smike, on the
night after the letter had been dispatched.

"Not I!" rejoined Nicholas, with assumed
gaiety, for the confession would have made the
boy miserable all night; "I was thinking about
my sister, Smike."

"Sister!"

"Ay."

"Is she like you?" inquired Smike.

"Why, so they say," replied Nicholas,
laughing, "only a great deal handsomer."

"She must be *very* beautiful," said Smike,
after thinking a little while with his hands
folded together, and his eyes bent upon his
friend.

"Anybody who did n't know you as well as
I do, my dear fellow, would say you were an
accomplished courtier," said Nicholas.

"I don't even know what that is," replied Smike, shaking his head. "Shall I ever see your sister?"

. . . .

At Newman Noggs's darkly worded summons the pair now return to London — Nicholas saying, "Heaven knows I have remained here for the best, and sorely against my own will; but even now I may have dallied too long. What can have happened? Smike, my good fellow, here — take my purse. Put our things together, and pay what little debts we owe — quick, and we shall be in time for the morning coach. I will only tell them that we are going, and will return to you immediately."

Not quite in keeping. Very few mental defectives can make change and pay bills.

The unhappy event of Smike's being discovered takes place soon after this return to London:

"He had been gazing for a long time through a jeweller's window, wishing he could take some of the beautiful trinkets home as a present, and imagining what delight they would afford if he could, when the clocks struck three-quarters

past eight; roused by the sound, he hurried on
at a very quick pace, and was crossing the
corner of a by-street when he felt himself violently brought to, with a jerk so sudden that
he was obliged to cling to a lamp-post to save
himself from falling. At the same moment, a
small boy clung tight round his leg, and a shrill
cry of 'Here he is, father! Hooray!' vibrated
in his ears.

"Smike knew that voice too well. He cast his
despairing eyes downward towards the form
from which it had proceeded, and, shuddering
from head to foot, looked round. Mr. Squeers
had hooked him in the coat-collar with the
handle of his umbrella, and was hanging on at
the other end with all his might and main.
The cry of triumph proceeded from Master
Wackford, who, regardless of all his kicks and
struggles, clung to him with the tenacity of
a bull-dog."

Smike, however, escaped from his old tor-
mentors and made his way to Newman Noggs,
who received him and wished to keep him for
the night, "but, as Smike would not hear of this
— pleading his anxiety to see his friends again
— they eventually sallied forth together; and

the night being, by this time, far advanced, and Smike being, besides, so footsore that he could hardly crawl along, it was within an hour of sunrise when they reached their destination.

"At the first sound of their voices outside the house, Nicholas, who had passed a sleepless night, devising schemes for the recovery of his lost charge, started from his bed, and joyfully admitted them. There was so much noisy conversation, and congratulation, and indignation, that the remainder of the family were soon awakened, and Smike received a warm and cordial welcome, not only from Kate, but from Mrs. Nickleby."

Of the further clumsy efforts to capture Smike by Mr. Squeers through Mr. Snawley (who pretends to be Smike's father), little need be said. It will be remembered that Nicholas and the efficient John Browdie take decisive proceedings, which are a great credit to their muscular training. Ralph Nickleby, the greatest villain of all, here appears in the company of the other villains.

The story now draws to a close. In spite of the care and kindness lavished upon him,

"Smike became alarmingly ill; so reduced and exhausted that he could scarcely move from room to room without assistance; and so worn and emaciated, that it was painful to look upon him. Nicholas was warned, by the same medical authority to whom he had at first appealed, that the last chance and hope of his life depended on his being instantly removed from London. That part of Devonshire in which Nicholas had been himself bred was named as the most favourable spot; but this advice was cautiously coupled with the information that whoever accompanied him thither must be prepared for the worst; for every token of rapid consumption had appeared, and he might never return alive."

And the kind Cheeryble brothers provide for him as they provide for every one, and Nicholas and the poor boy go to the country.

"They procured a humble lodging in a small farmhouse, surrounded by meadows, where Nicholas had often revelled when a child with a troop of merry school fellows; and here they took up their rest.

"At first Smike was strong enough to walk about, for short distances at a time, with no other support or aid than that which Nicholas could afford him. At this time nothing appeared to interest him so much as visiting those places which had been most familiar to his friend in bygone days. Yielding to this fancy and pleased to find that its indulgence beguiled the sick boy of many tedious hours, and never failed to afford him matter for thought and conversation afterwards, Nicholas made such spots the scenes of their daily rambles; driving him from place to place in a little pony-chair, and supporting him on his arm while they walked slowly among these old haunts, or lingered in the sunlight to take long parting looks of those which were most quiet and beautiful."

It was at this time that Smike saw the man who had taken him to Dotheboys Hall, and remembered with terror his evil face —

"He stood leaning upon his stick and looking at me, exactly as I told you I remembered him. He was dusty with walking, and poorly dressed, — I think his clothes were ragged, — but directly I saw him, the wet night, his face when he left me, the parlour I was left in, and the people who were there, all seemed to come back together. When he knew I saw him, he looked frightened; for he started, and shrunk away. I have thought of him by day and dreamt of him by night. He looked in my sleep when I was quite a little child, and has looked in my sleep ever since, as he did just now."

"And now Nicholas began to see that hope was gone, and that, upon the partner of his poverty, and the sharer of his better fortune, the world was closing fast. There was little pain, little uneasiness, but there was no rallying, no effort, no struggle for life. He was worn and wasted to the last degree; his voice had sunk so low, that he could scarce be heard to speak. Nature was thoroughly exhausted, and he had lain him down to die.

"Nicholas learnt for the first time that the dying boy, with all the ardour of a nature concentrated on one absorbing, hopeless, secret passion, loved his sister Kate.

"He had procured a lock of her hair, which hung at his breast, folded in one or two slight ribands she had worn. He prayed that, when he was dead, Nicholas would take it off, so that no eyes but his might see it, and that when he was laid in his coffin and about to be placed in the earth, he would hang it round his neck again, that it might rest with him in the grave.

"Upon his knees Nicholas gave him this pledge, and promised again that he should rest in the spot he had pointed out. They embraced, and kissed each other on the cheek.

"Now," he murmured, "I am happy."

"He fell into a light slumber, and waking smiled as before; then spoke of beautiful gardens, which he said stretched out before him, and were filled with figures of men, women, and many children, all with light upon their faces; then whispered that it was Eden — and so died."

Pathetic and beautiful as the skill of the great writer has made this picture, who shall say that it is wholly without foundation? Yet truth compels us to add that such regard to the future and to the organization of human life and its innermost meaning, is all but unknown to the mental defective.

For all that, Smike in some ways is the greatest study of a mental defective in English literature. And the greatest lesson for us is that it is our duty to protect feeble-minded persons from being exploited and cruelly treated as Squeers treated Smike.

"The grass was green above the dead boy's grave, and trodden by feet so small and light, that not a daisy drooped its head beneath their pressure. Through all the spring and summer time, garlands of fresh flowers, wreathed by infant hands, rested on the stone; and when the children came to change them lest they should wither and be pleasant to him no longer, their eyes filled with tears, and they spoke low and softly. . . ."

Our Mutual Friend

Many readers conclude at once that Sloppy is mentally defective. Not proven. He was probably normal.

Sloppy — so called, it is said, because he was found on a sloppy day. Sloppy was a beautiful newspaper reader.

"You might n't think it, but Sloppy is a beautiful reader of a newspaper. He, do the Police in different voices."

"Of an ungainly make was Sloppy. Too much of him longwise, too little of him broadwise, and too many sharp angles of him angle-

wise. One of those shambling male human creatures born to be indiscreetly candid in the reve-
lation of buttons; every button he had about
him glaring at the public to a quite preter-
natural extent. A considerable capital of knee
and elbow and wrist and ankle, had Sloppy,
and he did n't know how to dispose of it to the
best advantage, but was always investing it in
wrong securities, and so getting himself into em-
barrassed circumstances. Full-Private Number
One in the Awkward Squad of the rank and
file of life was Sloppy, and yet had his glimmer-
ing notions of standing true to the Colours."

His remarks are not lacking in intelligence,
and some of his peculiarities in regard to buttons and other things may be accounted for
by the peculiarities of the gifted writer who
created him. On the other hand, the sense of
humor and reasoning power which he shows
on more than one occasion, as well as his capa-
bilities, are all to the good.

"'He would have made a wonderful cabinet-
maker,' said Mrs. Higden, 'if there had been
the money to put him to it.' She had seen him
handle tools that he had borrowed to mend the
mangle, or to knock a broken piece of furniture

together, in a surprising manner. As to con-
structing toys for the Minders out of nothing,
he had done that daily. And once as many as a
dozen people had got together in the lane to see
the neatness with which he fitted the broken
pieces of a foreign monkey's musical instrument.
'That's well,' said the Secretary. 'It will not be
hard to find a trade for him.'"

To be sure, there are many mental defectives
who can do these things, but Sloppy seems to
have done them with little or no supervision,
and that is a very different thing. Besides, the
poor lad is capable of self-reproach. It is very
seldom, if ever, that a mental defective is
capable of self-reproach.

When Mrs. Betty Higden was buried —

"I've took it in my head," said Sloppy, laying it, inconsolable, against the church door,
when all was done — "I've took it in my
wretched head that I might have sometimes
turned a little harder for her, and it cuts me
deep to think so now."

"The Reverend Frank Milvey, comforting
Sloppy, expounded to him how the best of us
were more or less remiss in our turnings at our
respective mangles — some of us very much

so — and how we were all a halting, failing, feeble, and inconstant crew.

"*She* warn't, sir," said Sloppy, taking this ghostly counsel rather ill, in behalf of his late benefactress. "Let us speak for ourselves, sir. She went through with whatever duty she had to do. She went through with me, she went through with the Minders, she went through with herself, she went through with everythink. O, Mrs. Higden, Mrs. Higden, you was a woman and a mother and a mangler in a million million."

"With those heartfelt words Sloppy removed his dejected head from the church door, and took it back to the grave in the corner, and laid it down there, and wept alone. 'Not a very poor grave,' said the Reverend Frank Milvey, brushing his hand across his eyes, 'when it has that homely figure on it. Richer, I think, than it could be made by most of the sculpture in Westminster Abbey.'

"They left him undisturbed, and passed out at the wicket-gate."

For Sloppy's sense of humor —

"No, nor *I* ain't gone," said another voice.

"Somebody else had come in quietly by the folding doors. Turning his head, Wegg beheld

his persecutor, the ever-wakeful dustman,
accoutred with fantail hat and velveteen smalls
complete. Who, untying his tied-up broken
head, revealed a head that was whole, and a
face that was Sloppy's.

"Ha, ha, ha, gentlemen!" roared Sloppy, in
a peal of laughter, and with immeasurable
relish. "He never thought as I could sleep
standing, and often done it when I turned for
Mrs. Higden! He never thought as I used to
give Mrs. Higden the Police-news in different
voices! But I did lead him a life all through it,
gentlemen, I hope I really and truly DID!"
Here Mr. Sloppy opening his mouth to a quite
alarming extent, and throwing back his head
to peal again, revealed incalculable buttons.

"Oh!" said Wegg, slightly discomfited, but
not much as yet; "one and one is two not dis-
missed, is it? Bof — fin! Just let me ask a
question. Who set this chap on, in this dress,
when the carting began? Who employed this
fellow?"

"I say!" remonstrated Sloppy, jerking his
head forward. "No fellows, or I'll throw you
out of winder!" . . .

"The words were but out of his mouth when

John Harmon lifted his finger, and Sloppy, who was now close to Wegg, backed to Wegg's back, stooped, grasped his coat collar behind with both hands, and deftly swung him up like the sack of flour or coals before mentioned. A countenance of special discontent and amazement Mr. Wegg exhibited in this position, with his buttons almost as prominently on view as Sloppy's own, and with his wooden leg in a highly unaccommodating state. But not for many seconds was his countenance visible in the room; for Sloppy lightly trotted out with him and trotted down the staircase, Mr. Venus attending to open the street door. Mr. Sloppy's instructions had been to deposit his burden in the road; but a scavenger's cart happening to stand unattended at the corner, with its little ladder planted against the wheel, Mr. S. found it impossible to resist the temptation of shooting Mr. Silas Wegg into the cart's contents. A somewhat difficult feat, achieved with great dexterity, and with a prodigious splash."

Sloppy could find work for himself —
"I could make you," said Sloppy, surveying the room, — "I could make you a handy set of

nests to lay the dolls in. Or I could make you a handy little set of drawers, to keep your silks and threads and scraps in. Or I could turn you a rare handle for that crutch-stick, if it belongs to him you call your father."

"It belongs to me," returned the little creature, with a quick flush of her face and neck. "I am lame."

"Poor Sloppy flushed too, for there was an instinctive delicacy behind his buttons, and his own hand had struck it. He said, perhaps, the best thing in the way of amends that could be said. "I am very glad it's yours, because I'd rather ornament it for you than for any one else. Please may I look at it?"

Sloppy's mental capital was, after all, by no means insignificant. It is scarcely likely that Dickens intended him to be a mental defective.

DOMBEY AND SON

Mr. Edwin Percy Whipple, in his Introduction to "Dombey and Son," says: "Toots must be considered one of Dickens's most delicious characterizations, in that domain of character in which he preëminently excelled, namely, the representation of individuals in whom benevolence of feeling is combined with imperfection of intellect."

Mr. Whipple tells us in the same paragraph that "Owing to excessive cramming, he (Toots) began, as soon as he had whiskers, to leave off having brains." With this view of Mr. Toots's mental condition, we can hardly agree in these days. He was one of the high-grade mental defectives whose feeble-mindedness does not become unmistakable until the time arrives when they ought to begin to bear the real responsibility of life — to be "grown-up" as the common phrase has it. But Mr. Toots belongs to the class who do not quite grow up. At the "awkward age" for boys and girls, somewhere between boyhood and manhood, or girlhood and womanhood, when some foolish word or action disturbs their parents, how often have we heard the father or mother express the wish and hope that their offspring would soon "get more sense." Normal boys and girls do "get more sense."

You shall hardly be able to recognize Young Hopeful three years from now — when he has found himself. It was only an awkward fluttering when he tried the first few flights from the parent nest. He is all right before long. But the Mr. Toots type never "gets more sense."

We meet Mr. Toots when we go to Dr. Blimber's School in company with little Paul Dombey. Mr. Toots is overgrown and employs himself in blushing and chuckling. He shows himself kindly disposed to Paul when they meet again in the schoolroom, but he cannot get the name "Dombey and Son" into his mind, and says he will ask Paul to mention the name again to-morrow morning. This is so that he can write himself a letter from Dombey and Son immediately. This, of course, is the accomplishment for which Dickens has made Toots famous — writing letters to himself. We often see him at this occupation in the course of the story. But we never hear him say a really sensible word:

"How are you?" he would say to Paul fifty times a day.

"Quite well, sir, thank you," Paul would answer. "Shake hands," would be Toots's next advance. Which Paul, of course, would immediately do. Mr. Toots generally said again, after a long interval of staring and hard breathing,

"How are you?" To which Paul again replied, "Quite well, sir, thank you."

Every sensible person must pay proper attention to dress. But Mr. Toots pays a foolish attention to it. At the school party — "Mr. Toots was one blaze of jewellery and buttons; and he felt the circumstance so strongly that . . . he took Paul aside, and said, 'What do you think of this, Dombey!'

"But notwithstanding this modest confidence in himself, Mr. Toots appeared to be involved in a good deal of uncertainty whether, on the whole, it was judicious to button the bottom button of his waistcoat, and whether on a calm revision of all the circumstances, it was best to wear his wrist-bands turned up or turned down. Observing that Mr. Feeder's were turned up, Mr. Toots turned his up; but the wrist-bands of the next arrival being turned down, Mr. Toots turned his down. The differences in point of waistcoat buttoning, not only at the bottom, but at the top too, became so numerous and complicated as the arrivals thickened, that Mr. Toots was continually fingering that article of dress, as if he were performing on some instrument, and appearing to find the incessant execution it demanded quite bewildering."

When raw materials are under consideration and that distinguished commercial gentleman, Mr. Baps, attempts to ask Mr. Toots what should be done with raw materials when they came into your ports in return for your drain of gold, Mr. Toots is quite capable of replying — "Cook 'em."

Mr. Toots's conversation, when he calls on Florence after Paul Dombey's death is a perfect example, for the most part, of the conversation of a feeble-minded person.

"You were very kind to my dear brother," said Florence. . . .

"Oh, it's of no consequence," said Mr. Toots, hastily. "Warm, ain't it?" And so on and so on.

"Nothing seemed to do Mr. Toots so much good as incessantly leaving cards at Mr. Dombey's door. No tax-gatherer in the British Dominions — that wide-spread territory on which the sun never sets, and where the tax-gatherer never goes to bed — was more regular and persevering in his calls than Mr. Toots.

"Mr. Toots never went upstairs; and always

performed the same ceremonies, richly-dressed
for the purpose, at the hall-door."

At length Mr. Toots manages to get inside
the hall-door and attempted to kiss Florence
Dombey's maid, the ever alert Miss Susan
Nipper.

"Go along with you," exclaimed Susan, giving him a push. "Innocents like you, too!
Who'll begin next! Go along, sir!" Thereupon
the cheering scene follows in which Diogenes,
the dog, seizes Mr. Toots by the leg, and Mr.
Carker comes to the rescue.

Mr. Toots falls into the clutches of the Game
Chicken, "the celebrated public character who
had covered himself and his country with glory
in his contest with the Nobby Shropshire One."
The ex-prize fighter, though perhaps not of a
very high order of intelligence, knows enough
to recognize Mr. Toots as a gold mine, and to
make a good living out of him, Mr. Toots being
by no means able to take care either of himself
or his money. The Game Chicken is "jealous
of his ascendancy" and tries to keep every one
else away from Toots. However, Captain Cut-
tle, and above all, Florence, are not forgotten
by Mr. Toots. Toots knows that Florence is

an angel, and frequently says so. He says to Captain Gills, "If I could be dyed black, and made into Miss Dombey's slave, I would consider it a compliment."

When Susan Nipper rejoins her mistress after their cruel separation, she has evidently learned somewhat more of Mr. Toots's character —

"I — I — I — never did see such a creetur as that Toots," said Susan, "in all my born days, never!"

" . . . He may not be a Solomon," pursued the Nipper, with her usual volubility, "nor do I say he is, but this I do say, a less selfish human creature human nature never knew!"

After the interview with Florence in which Toots takes farewell of her, having learned of her approaching marriage to "Lieutenant Walters," an interview in which the sweet and kind ways and words of Florence comfort even the dejected Mr. Toots, that gentleman prevails upon Susan Nipper to accompany him to church in order to hear the banns for Florence and the Lieutenant.

This and other small indications prepare us somewhat for the scene in which Mr. and Mrs. Toots (*née* Nipper) call upon Dr. Blimber.

The closing scene in which Mr. Toots appears in this book is at the Midshipman.

"Mr. Toots's face is very red as he bursts into the little parlour."

"Captain Gills," says Mr. Toots, "and Mr. Sols, I am happy to inform you that Mrs. Toots has had an increase to her family. . . . We're positively getting on, you know. There's Florence and Susan and now here's another little stranger."

"A female stranger?" inquires the Captain.

"Yes, Captain Gills," says Mr. Toots, "and I'm glad of it. The oftener we can repeat that most extraordinary woman, my opinion is, the better."

True. But what would poor Susan think when Florence and little Susan and the other little stranger perhaps turned out as "innocentest" as their father. Toots may be amusing. He had money to help to make him so, and Dickens to make us see him so. But the burden of the feeble-minded and their children in modern real life is not amusing, but tragic and awful.

BLEAK HOUSE

An authority on Dickens once told me that "Jo" in "Bleak House" was perhaps the best example of a mental defective in Dickens's works. "Of course there is 'Jo' in 'Bleak House,'" he said. He had forgotten, for the moment, that it is possible for a poor boy, unfortunate, untaught, uncared-for, and utterly neglected, to be thought mentally defective when he is really normal. There is a character in "Bleak House" who is a mental defective, but it is poor "Guster." "Jo" is not mentally defective.

"Guster, really aged three or four and twenty, but looking a round ten years older, goes cheap with this unaccountable drawback of fits; and is so apprehensive of being returned on the hands of her patron saint that except when she is found with her head in the pail, or the sink, or the copper, or the dinner, or anything else that happens to be near her at the time of her seizure, she is always at work. She is a satisfaction to the parents and guardians of the 'Prentices, who feel that there is little danger of her inspiring tender emotions in the

breast of youth; she is a satisfaction to Mrs.
Snagsby, who can always find fault with her;
she is a satisfaction to Mr. Snagsby, who thinks
it a charity to keep her. The law stationer's
establishment is, in Guster's eyes, a temple of
plenty and splendour. She believes the little
drawing-room upstairs, always kept, as one
may say, with its hair in papers and its pina-
fore on, to be the most elegant apartment
in Christendom. The view it commands of
Cook's Court at one end (not to mention a
squint into Cursitor Street) and of Coavinses
the sheriff's officer's back yard at the other, she
regards as a prospect of unequalled beauty.
The portraits it displays in oil — and plenty
of it, too — of Mr. Snagsby looking at Mrs.
Snagsby, and of Mrs. Snagsby looking at Mr.
Snagsby, are in her eyes as achievements of
Raphael or Titian. Guster has some recom-
penses for her many privations."

Jo appears first at the inquest upon a man
who died unknown. Mrs. Piper deposed —
"Never see him speak to neither child nor
grown person at any time (excepting the boy
that sweeps the crossing down the lane over the
way round the corner which if he was here

would tell you that he has been seen a speaking to him frequent)" — so the boy is sent for.

"Name, Jo. Nothing else that he knows on. Don't know that everybody has two names. Never heard of sich a think. Don't know that Jo is short for a longer name. Thinks it long enough for *him*. *He* don't find no fault with it. Spell it? No. *He* can't spell it. No father, no mother, no friends. Never been to school. What's home? Knows a broom's a broom, and knows it's wicked to tell a lie. Don't recollect who told him about the broom, or about the lie, but knows both. Can't exactly say what'll be done to him arter he's dead if he tells a lie to the gentlemen here, but believes it'll be something wery bad to punish him, and serve him right — and so he'll tell the truth."

Jo's account of himself to the Coroner is —

"That one cold winter night, when he, the boy, was shivering in a doorway near his crossing, the man turned to look at him, and came back, and, having questioned him and found that he had not a friend in the world, said, 'Neither have I. Not one!' and gave him the price of a supper and a night's lodging. That the man had often spoken to him since; and

asked him whether he slept sound at night, and
how he bore cold and hunger, and whether he
ever wished to die; and similar strange ques-
tions. That when the man had no money, he
would say in passing, 'I am as poor as you
to-day, Jo'; but that when he had any, he had
always (as the boy most heartily believes) been
glad to give him some.

"He wos wery good to me," says the boy,
wiping his eyes with his wretched sleeve.
"Wen I see him a layin' so stritched out just
now, I wished he could have heerd me tell him
so. He wos wery good to me, he wos!" . . .

"Mr. Snagsby, lying in wait for him, puts a
half-crown in his hand. 'If ever you see me coming past your crossing with my little woman
— I mean a lady' — says Mr. Snagsby, with
his finger on his nose, 'don't allude to it!'"

Jo has imagination. The mentally defective
have imagination sometimes but not often.
Would a mental defective perform such an act
as this?

"With the night comes a slouching figure
through the tunnel-court, to the outside of the
iron gate. It holds the gate with its hands, and

looks in between the bars; stands looking in, for a little while.

"It then, with an old broom it carries, softly sweeps the step, and makes the archway clean. It does so, very busily and trimly; looks in again, a little while; and so departs.

"Jo, is it thou? Well, well! Though a rejected witness, who 'can't exactly say' what will be done to him in greater hands than men's, thou art not quite in outer darkness. There is something like a distant ray of light in thy muttered reason for this: —

"'He wos wery good to me, he wos!' . . . .

"A band of music comes and plays. Jo listens to it. So does a dog — a drover's dog, waiting for his master outside a butcher's shop, and evidently thinking about those sheep he has had upon his mind for some hours, and is happily rid of. He seems perplexed respecting three or four; can't remember where he left them; looks up and down the street, as half expecting to see them astray; suddenly pricks up his ears and remembers all about it. A thoroughly vagabond dog, accustomed to low company and public houses; a terrific dog to sheep; ready at a whistle to scamper over their backs, and tear out mouthfuls of their wool; but an educated, improved, developed dog, who has been taught his duties and knows how to discharge them. He and Jo listen to the music, probably with much the same amount of animal satisfaction; likewise, as to awakened association, aspiration or regret, melancholy or joyful reference to things beyond the senses, they are probably upon a par. But otherwise, how far above the human listener is the brute!

"Turn that dog's descendants wild, like Jo, and in a very few years they will so degenerate that they will lose even their bark — but not their bite."

Jo appears next as a guide to Lady Dedlock, when, in disguise, she visits the places mentioned in the account of the inquest appearing in the newspapers.

Poor Jo is moved on by the arbitrary and cruel constable, but this incident gives us evidence of the real mental powers that he possessed —

"You are very poor, ain't you?" says the constable.

"Yes, I am, indeed, sir, wery poor in gin'ral," replies Jo.

"I leave you to judge now! I shook these two half-crowns out of him," says the constable, producing them to the company, "in only putting my hand upon him!"

"They're wot's left, Mr. Snagsby," said Jo, "out of a sov'ring as wos given me by a lady in a wale as sed she wos a servant and as come to my crossin' one night and asked to be showd this 'ere ouse and the ouse wot him as you giv the writin' to died at, and the berrin-ground wot he's berrid in. She ses to me she ses 'are you the boy at the Inkwhich?' she ses. I ses 'yes' I ses. She ses to me she ses 'can you show me all them places?' I ses 'yes I can' I ses. And she ses to me 'do it' and I dun it and she giv me a sov'ring and hooked it. And I ain't had much of the sov'ring neither," says Jo, with dirty tears, "fur I had to pay five bob, down in Tom-all-alone's, afore they'd square it fur to giv me change, and then a young man he thieved another five while I was asleep and another boy he thieved nine-pence and the landlord he stood drains round with a lot more on it."

"You don't expect anybody to believe this, about the lady and the sovereign, do you?" says the constable, eyeing him aside with ineffable disdain.

"I don't know as I do, sir," replies Jo. "I don't expect nothink at all, sir, much, but that's the true hist'ry on it."

It is well known that seldom, indeed, can mental defectives manage to make change. Jo probably could have learned a great deal if he had had an opportunity. He had no schooling. His power of recognition of persons is not so much to the point, although it is sufficiently wonderful in its way. Mental defectives often possess such powers, and like children they frequently are remarkable judges of character.

Had the plot of the story permitted us to know more of Jo's early history, or of his development, it would have been easier to pronounce him normal, or possibly, on the other hand, mentally defective. But judging from what we are told, he does not appear to be mentally defective.

CHAPTER III

BULWER LYTTON: CHARLES READE: VICTOR
HUGO: GEORGE MACDONALD: GEORGE ELIOT:
JOSEPH CONRAD: ROBERT
LOUIS STEVENSON

BULWER LYTTON — ERNEST MALTRAVERS

IN "Ernest Maltravers" and the sequel "Alice," Bulwer Lytton introduces a beautiful girl who is evidently regarded by her father as mentally defective. These two novels are not only a romance, but a romance *de luxe* as it were. Ernest falls in love and goes through all the beautiful and distracting experiences of such a state, not once but four times, so that the reader is not deprived of his rights in any possible particular.

This is a book which should be read in early youth, when it is possible to believe everything, even that Alice Darvil could have been so charming and beautiful and desirable and yet be the daughter of one of the worst villains ever created by the imagination of the gifted author. Of course the villain meets his death at the proper moment.

Alice is thus described when she is introduced to the reader:

"She seemed about fifteen years of age; and her complexion was remarkably pure and delicate, even despite the sunburnt tinge which her habits of toil had brought it. Her auburn hair hung in loose and natural curls over her forehead, and its luxuriance was remarkable even in one so young. Her countenance was beautiful, nay, even faultless, in its small and childlike features; but the expression pained you, — it was so vacant. In repose it was almost the expression of an idiot; but when she spoke or smiled, or even moved a muscle, the eyes, color, lips, kindled into life which proved that the intellect was still there, though but imperfectly awakened."

"I did not steal any, father," she said, in a quiet voice; "but I should like to have taken some only I knew you would beat me if I did."

"And what do you want money for?"

"To get food when I'm hungered."

The author wisely does not commit himself to the statement that Alice was mentally defective, but there is, as the reader will have already concluded, much reason to consider that, in the author's opinion, she was mentally defective.

The appearance of Ernest Maltravers has the effect of beginning the awakening of her mind according to the story. This "awakening" cannot happen when the mind is really defective, because that defect is chiefly shown in the absence of the power to develop and learn.

Alice shows a good deal of sense and discretion in assisting Ernest to make his escape, and when she meets him by chance afterwards, there begins that interest and affection between them which is the main thread in the story.

Finding that Alice has been ill-used because she helped him to escape, and that she is quite destitute, having run away from her father's ill-treatment, Maltravers, with platonic intentions, arranged for Alice to live in a cottage with him and engaged an old woman as a servant. Thinking it prudent to conceal his name, he adopted the name of Butler, and devoted himself during his residence in this place to teaching Alice music. Her accomplishment in this direction and others, in which Mr. Simcox

is her teacher, practically settles the question
as to whether or not she is mentally defective.
Indeed, we learn later on in the story that she
was to earn her own living by giving lessons in
music. This a mentally defective person would
not have been able to do.

The scene of the hero's adventures now
changes and Alice temporarily disappears
from the story, but the consequences of the
romance skillfully interwoven with the story
are of unusual interest.

The unfortunate Alice is discovered by her
father and escapes from him once more, after
many trials and many difficulties. The cottage
where she and Ernest were so happy together
is improved beyond recognition by a new
tenant so that all trace of their residence is lost.

A good Samaritan now appears upon the
scene in the person of the charitable Mrs. Leslie,
and indeed it is Mrs. Leslie who arranges for
Alice to take up her abode with a music-master
where Alice earns her own living.

Mr. Templeton, a banker, meeting her and
being charmed by her, wishes to make better
arrangements for her, but Alice declines —

"Because," said Alice, almost solemnly,

"there are some hours when I feel I must be alone. I sometimes think I am not all right *here*," and she touched her forehead. "They called me an idiot before I knew *him!* No, I could not live with others, for I can only cry when nobody but my child is with me."

Later on Mr. Templeton insists on her marrying him, but she does so only upon condition that she remains his wife in name alone.

Once Ernest sees her when some one has persuaded him to go to hear a celebrated preacher —

"The dim outline of a female form, in the distance, riveted the eyes and absorbed the thoughts of Maltravers. The chapel was darkened, though it was broad daylight; and the face of the person that attracted Ernest's attention was concealed by her head-dress and veil. But that bend of the neck, so simply graceful, so humbly modest, recalled to his heart but one image. Every one has, perhaps, observed that there is a physiognomy (if the bull may be pardoned) of form as well as face, which it rarely happens that two persons possess in common. And this, with most, is peculiarly marked in the turn of the head, the outline of the shoulders, and the ineffable something that characterizes the postures of each individual in repose. The more intently he gazed, the more firmly Ernest was persuaded that he saw before him the long-lost, the never-to-be-forgotten mistress of his boyish days, and his first love."

He was unable to find her afterwards. The above description is quoted because it becomes evident that it is not the description of one who is a mental defective.

ALICE

The second volume "Alice" contains but little allusion to Alice herself. She appears, it is true, in the first chapter, along with Mrs. Leslie, in a charming scene, of which she is herself the chief charm. The skillful interweaving of the author's interesting and intricate plot cannot be further referred to here.

The unknown Alice becomes Lady Vargrave by these ways which are so uniformly successful in novels but not always in real life. Alice never, however, forgets Ernest, and one of the interesting wiles of the author which keeps alive our attention and pleasure is that she does not know Ernest as Maltravers, but only as Butler.

Later on in the story some one called Butler begins to be known as an author.

The curate, one of her best friends, who knows her history, says of this writer:

"He must have a spell in his works that I have not discovered; for at times it seems to operate even on you."

"Because," said Lady Vargrave, "they remind me of *his* conversation, *his* habits of thought."

"And if," said the curate curiously, — "if, now that you are free, you were ever to meet with *him* again, and his memory had been as faithful as yours; and if he offered the sole atonement in his power for all that his early error cost you, — if such a chance should happen in the vicissitudes of life, you would —"

"The curate stopped short; for he was struck by the exceeding paleness of his friend's cheek and the tremor of her delicate frame.

"If that were to happen," said she, in a very low voice; "if we were to meet again, and if he were — as you and Mrs. Leslie seem to think — poor, and like myself, humbly born; if my fortune could assist him; if my love could still — changed, altered, as I am — ah, do not talk of it, — I cannot bear the thought of happiness! And yet, if before I die I *could* but see him again!"

"She clasped her hands fervently as she spoke, and the blush that overspread her face threw over it so much of bloom and freshness that even Evelyn at that moment would scarcely have seemed more young.

"Enough," she added, after a little while, as the glow died away. "It is but a foolish hope; all earthly love is buried; and my heart is there!"

"She pointed to the heavens, and both were silent."

In the end all the villains receive their deserts and the heroes and heroines their just rewards, and Alice and her lover, in spite of many threatening clouds, appear at the end united, and with the sun of happiness shining upon them.

"Maltravers rose, and they stood before each other, face to face. And how lovely still was Alice, — lovelier, he thought, even than of old! And those eyes, so divinely blue, so dove-like and soft, yet with some spiritual and un-fathomable mystery in their clear depth, were once more fixed upon him. Alice seemed turned to stone; she moved not; she spoke not, — she scarcely breathed; she gazed spellbound as if her senses — as if life itself — had deserted her.

"Alice!" murmured Maltravers, — "Alice, we meet at last!"

His voice restored memory, consciousness, youth, at once to her. She uttered a long cry of unspeakable joy, of rapture! . . . and said passionately, "I have been true to thee! I have been true to thee, or this hour would have killed me!"

The interest of this romantic story may perhaps be heightened by the device of representing the hero as able to "cure" a mentally defective person, but this is a device that can no longer be used by novelists, since it is an impossibility and cannot happen in real life. This heroine was never mentally defective.

CHARLES READE — PUT YOURSELF IN HIS PLACE

In order to interest the public in the protection of the file-cutters and grinders who suffered so much from lead poisoning, and because he saw how many valuable lives were sacrificed and how many good workmen had their health broken, Charles Reade drew his pen "against cowardly assassination and sordid tyranny."

The last sentence in the book is this: "I have taken a few undeniable truths, out of many, and have laboured to make my readers realize those appalling facts of the day, which most men know, but not one in a thousand comprehends, and not one in a hundred thousand realizes, until Fiction — which, whatever you may have been told to the contrary, is the highest, widest, noblest, and greatest of all the arts — comes to his aid, studies, penetrates, digests, the hard facts of chronicles and blue-books, and makes their dry bones live."

Improvements and safeguards against disease, and especially against lead poisoning, which Charles Reade describes in the "Report of Henry Little," have long been put into operation and lead poisoning is rapidly becoming a thing of the past.

Henry Little is, of course, the chief character in the book and a Good Samaritan, Dr. Amboyne, induces Henry Little to devote his ability to the study of lead poisoning and the preparation of this "Report."

Dr. Amboyne's favorite phrase, "Put yourself in his place," gives the book its name.

When Henry Little visits Dr. Amboyne at his office he finds him in his study, "teaching what looked a boy of sixteen, but was twenty-two, to read monosyllables. On Little's entrance the pupil retired from his up-hill work, and glowered with vacillating eyes. The lad had a fair feminine face, with three ill things in it; a want, a wildness, and a weakness. To be sure Henry saw it at a disadvantage; for vivid intelligence would come now and then across this mild, wild, vacant face, like the breeze that sweeps a farmyard pond."

Henry remarks that this boy, who is to be his fellow-worker, "does not look up to much," and the Doctor replies, "Never mind; he can beat the town at one or two things, and it is for these we will use him. Some call him an idiot. The expression is neat and vigorous, but not precise; so I have christened him the Anomaly. Anomaly, this is Mr. Little; go and shake hands with him, and admire him."

This is a truth that is far too often passed

over in work with the feeble-minded — They can often "beat the town" at something. If we can only find out what that something is and set them at it then our problems are largely solved.

Henry asks the Anomaly, "What is your real name, my man?"

"Silly Billy."

"Oh, then I am afraid you can't do much to help me."

"Oh, yes, I can, because —"

"Because what?"

"Because I like you."

"Well, that's lucky, anyway."

"Billy can catch trout when nobody else can," said the youngster, turning his eyes proudly up to Henry's.

Henry and his companion then proceed to Cheetham's works, and Henry begins his investigations among the dry grinders and razor-grinders and others.

"Up to this moment Silly Billy had fully justified that title. He had stuck to Henry's side like a dog, but with no more interest in the inquiry than a calf. Indeed, his wandering eye and vacant face had indicated that his scanty

wits were wool-gathering miles from the place
that contained his body.

"But as soon as he entered the saw-grinders'
room, his features lighted up, and his eye
kindled. He now took up a commanding position in the centre, and appeared to be listening
keenly. And he had not listened many seconds
before he cried out, 'There's the bad music!
there! there!' And he pointed to a grindstone
that was turning and doing its work exactly
like the others. 'Oh, the bad music!' cried
Billy. 'It is out of tune. It says, Murder!
murder! Out of tune!'

"Henry thought it his duty to inspect the
grindstone so vigorously denounced, and, naturally enough, went in front of the grinder.
But Billy pulled him violently to the side.
'You must n't stand there,' said he. 'That is
the way they fly when they break, and kill the
poor father, and then the mother lets down her
hair, and the boy goes crazed.'

"By this time the men were attracted by
the Anomaly's gestures and exclamations,
and several left their work, and came round
him. 'What is amiss, Billy? a flawed stone,
eh? Which is it?'

"Here! here!" said the boy. "This is the wheel of death. Kill it, break it, smash it, before it kills another father."

The story of Billy's life is told in the same chapter — that his father persisted in using such a flawed stone against warning and that Billy saw him killed by the stone and was afterwards an idiot. The narrative states that Billy was a very little boy at the time. We now know that even such a terrible tragedy as this cannot be the cause of mental defectiveness. This, however, is the only error in Charles Reade's study of a mental defective, and "Put yourself in His Place" was published nearly fifty years ago.

Henry now makes up his mind to take up the trade of wood-carving in addition to his own, and in this Billy is a valuable assistant, under the name of Rowbotham.

"Nor was Rowbotham a mere *nom de plume.* It was the real name of Silly Billy. The boy had some turn for carving, but was quite uncultivated. Henry took him into his employ, fed him and made free with his name.

"But Henry gave his apprentice, Billy, instruction, and the youth began to show an aptitude, which contrasted remarkably with his general incapacity."

Billy appears in the subsequent story very little, though occasional allusions to him occur. Thus, when Ransome, the Chief of Police, is deceived by the professional convict Shifty Dick, he emphasizes his disappointment by saying that Silly Billy, who smelt the faulty grindstone, would be very likely to be more successful in police work than Ransome himself was.

Those who are most successful in dealing with the feeble-minded are those who know that each one "can beat the town at one or two things," and who are clever enough, patient enough, and kind enough to find out in each case what these "one or two things" are and to supply the opportunity and the infinite praise and encouragement which often bring the work and output of the mental defective, under skilled supervision, almost to the level of the normal.

VICTOR HUGO — NOTRE DAME DE PARIS

Quasimodo, in "Notre Dame de Paris," has been thought by some readers to be mentally defective. But it is not so. In the very first scene where he is introduced and appears as "Pope of the Fools," Victor Hugo, having first described his sad physical defects, says that he has "with all this deformity, an indescribable and redoubtable air of vigor, agility, and courage." Such have not the feeble-minded. Vigor, agility, and courage, in that combination, they seldom or never possess. Quasimodo's power of self-control and inhibition is also evident. It appears in the second chapter, when he meets the priest who takes away from him his scepter and his brief sovereignty. These powers are not possessed by persons who are mentally defective.

But little information is given as to the childhood and youth of Quasimodo until we reach the first chapter of the Fourth Book, when we learn that sixteen years before the time of the story, in the year of Our Lord 1467, on Quasimodo Sunday, a poor deformed child was presented for charity on the wooden bed in the Church of Notre Dame opposite the great image of St. Christopher. The child appeared to be about four years old at that time. The parish priest, Monsieur Claude

Frollo, adopted the poor creature, put it in his cassock and carried it off.

"He baptized his adopted child, and gave him the name of Quasimodo, either because he desired thereby to mark the day when he had found him, or because he wished to designate by that name to what a degree the poor little creature was incomplete, and hardly sketched out. In fact, Quasimodo, one-eyed, hunchbacked, and knock-kneed, was only an 'Almost.'"

He developed and grew in mind and body "in sympathy with the cathedral."

"By dint of leaping, climbing, gamboling amid the abysses of the gigantic cathedral, he had become, in some sort, a monkey and a goat, like the Calabrian child who swims before he walks, and plays with the sea while still a babe.

"It was with great difficulty, and by dint of great patience that Claude Frollo had succeeded in teaching him to talk. But a fatality was attached to the poor foundling. Bellringer of Notre Dame at the age of fourteen, a new infirmity had come to complete his misfortunes: the bells had broken the drums of his ears; he had become deaf. The only gate which nature had left wide open for him had been abruptly closed, and forever."

The beautiful gypsy who showed humanity to poor Quasimodo when he was in chains on the pillory by detaching a gourd from her girdle and giving him to drink was the romance of Quasimodo's life.

"A big tear was seen to fall, and roll slowly down that deformed visage so long contracted with despair. It was the first in all probability the man had ever shed."

He had already tried to carry off the gypsy and he was able in the end to rescue her and place her within the precincts of the cathedral where she remained safe and well cared-for.

The tragedy which ends the story is well known, but there is quite sufficient evidence, for example, in the following passage, that whatever truth there may be in the legend introduced by Victor Hugo into his story, at least Quasimodo had mental powers exceeding those of the feeble-minded. Is it possible that there ever was a human life so tragic, filled with misfortunes so multiplied and heart-rending? One cannot bear to believe it.

The passage referred to is that which describes how the gypsy has been placed in safety in the cathedral, and on the following morning, on awaking at the same time with the sun, beheld at that window an object which frightened her, the unfortunate face of Quasimodo.

"She involuntarily closed her eyes again, but in vain; she fancied that she still saw through the rosy lids that gnome's mask.

"Then, while she still kept her eyes closed, she heard a rough voice saying, very gently:

"Be not afraid. I am your friend. I came to watch you sleep. It does not hurt you if I come to see you sleep, does it? What difference does it make to you if I am here when your eyes are closed! Now I am going. Stay, I have placed myself behind the wall. You can open your eyes again."

"There was something more plaintive than these words, and that was the accent in which they were uttered. The gypsy, much touched, opened her eyes. He was, in fact, no longer at the window. She approached the opening, and beheld the poor hunchback crouching in an angle of the wall, in a sad and resigned atti-

tude. She made an effort to surmount the repugnance with which he inspired her. 'Come,'
she said to him gently. From the movement
of the gypsy's lips Quasimodo thought that
she was driving him away; then he arose and
retired limping, slowly, with drooping head,
without even daring to raise to the young girl
his gaze full of despair. 'Do come,' she cried,
but he continued to retreat. Then she darted
from her cell, ran to him, and grasped his
arm.

"He was the first to break the silence. 'So
you were telling me to return?'

"She made an affirmative sign of the head,
and said, ʻ `ʼ

"Never have I seen my ugliness as at the
present moment. When I compare myself to
you, I feel a very great pity for myself, poor
unhappy monster that I am! Tell me, I must
look to you like a beast."

"Well!" she interposed with a smile, "tell
me why you saved me."

"He watched her attentively while she was
speaking.

"I understand," he replied. "You ask me
why I saved you. You have forgotten a wretch

who tried to abduct you one night, a wretch
to whom you rendered succour on the following day on their infamous pillory. A drop of
water and a little pity — that is more than I
can repay with my life. You have forgotten
that wretch, but he remembers it."

"She listened to him with profound tenderness. A tear swam in the eye of the bellringer,
but did not fall. He seemed to make it a sort
of point of honor to retain it.

"Listen," he resumed, when he was no
longer afraid that a tear would escape; "our
towers here are very high, a man who should
fall from them would be dead before touching
the pavement; when it shall please you to have
me fall, you will not have to utter even a
word, a glance will suffice."

"Then he arose. Unhappy as was the Bo-
hemian, this eccentric being still aroused some
compassion in her. She made him a sign to
remain.

"No, no," said he; "I must not remain too
long. I am not at my ease. It is out of pity that
you do not turn away your eyes. I shall go to
some place where I can see you without your
seeing me; it will be better so."

"He drew from his pocket a little metal whistle.

"Here," said he, "when you have need of me, when you wish me to come, when you will not feel too much horror at the sight of me, use this whistle. I can hear this sound."

"He laid the whistle on the floor and fled."

GEORGE MACDONALD — MALCOLM

In "Malcolm," and again in "Sir Gibbie," George MacDonald touches upon some of the problems connected with the life and care of mentally defective persons.

The hero of George MacDonald's "Malcolm" is an almost impossibly wonderful and attractive person.

"The Mad Laird," Mr. Stewart, first appears in the third chapter when Mistress Catanach, a very heavy female villain, is looking out to sea.

"While she thus stood, a strange figure drew near, approaching her with step almost as noiseless as that with which she had herself made her escape from Miss Horn's house. At a few yards' distance from her it stood, and gazed up at her countenance as intently as she

seemed to be gazing on the sea. It was a man
of dwarfish height and uncertain age, with a
huge hump upon his back, features of great
refinement, a long thin beard, and a forehead
unnaturally large, over eyes which, although
of a pale blue, mingled with a certain mottled
milky gleam, had a pathetic, dog-like expression. Decently dressed in black, he stood with
his hands in the pockets of his trousers,
gazing immovably in Mrs. Catanach's face."

Mrs. Catanach distresses the laird by her
vulgarity, and "the hunchback uttered a
shriek of dismay, and turned and fled; and as
he turned, long, thin, white hands flashed out
of his pockets, pressed against his ears, and
intertwined their fingers at the back of his
neck. With a marvellous swiftness he shot
down the steep descent towards the shore."

"The style she had given the hunchback
was no nickname. Stephen Stewart was laird
of the small property and ancient house of
Kirkbyres, of which his mother managed the
affairs, — hardly *for* her son, seeing that, beyond his clothes, and five pounds a year of
pocket-money, he derived no personal advantage from his possessions. He never went near

his own house, for, from some unknown reason, plentifully aimed at in the dark by the neighbours, he had such a dislike to his mother that he could not bear to hear the name of mother, or even the slightest allusion to the relationship.

"Some said he was a fool; others a madman; some both; none, however, said he was a rogue; and all would have been willing to allow that whatever it might be that caused the difference between him and other men, throughout the disturbing element blew ever and anon the air of a sweet humanity."

We meet the poor laird again in the seventh chapter, in which he is at the school, and very kindly treated by the schoolmaster, Mr. Graham.

But nothing calms the laird; he repeats in distress, "I dinna ken whaur I cam frae."

His mother, a beautiful but wicked and hard-hearted woman, is determined to shut him up in an asylum, and endeavors to deceive Malcolm into helping her. Malcolm acknowledges that the laird's mind is weak, but says, "His min', though cawpable o' a hantle mair nor a body wad think 'at didna ken him sae weel as I du, is certainly weyk — though maybe the weykness lies mair i' the tongue than i' the brain o' 'im after a' —"

His mother speaks of Stephen Stewart as an idiot, but Lady Florimel refers to him as a lunatic.

It must be remembered that the original meaning of lunatic included that of "idiot."

When the poor fellow was chased from his cave he took refuge in a garret. We have some description of his life there.

"In blessed compensation for much of the misery of his lot, the laird was gifted with an inborn delicate delight in nature and her ministrations such as few poets even possess; and this faculty was supplemented with a physical hardiness which, in association with his weakness and liability to certain appalling attacks, was truly astonishing. Though a rough hand might cause him exquisite pain, he could sleep soundly on the hardest floor; a hot room would induce a fit, but he would lie under an open window in the sharpest night without injury; a rude word would make him droop like a flower in frost, but he might go all day wet to the skin without taking cold. To all

kinds of what are called hardships, he had read-
ily become inured, without which it would
have been impossible for his love of nature to
receive such a full development. For hence he
grew capable of communion with her in all her
moods, undisabled either by the deadening
effects of present, or the aversion consequent
on past suffering. All the range of earth's shows,
from the grandeurs of sunrise or thunderstorm
down to the soft unfolding of a daisy or the
babbling birth of a spring, was to him an open
book. It is true, the delight of these things
was constantly mingled with, not unfrequently
broken, indeed, by the troublous question of
his origin; but it was only on occasions of
jarring contact with his fellows, that it was
accompanied by such agonies as my story has
represented. Sometimes he would sit on a
rock, murmuring the words over and over,
and dabbling his bare feet, small and deli-
cately formed, in the translucent green of a
tide-abandoned pool. But oftener in a soft
dusky wind, he might have been heard uttering
them gently and coaxingly, as if he would wile
from the evening zephyr the secret of his birth
—which surely mother Nature must know.

The confinement of such a man would have been in the highest degree cruel, and must speedily have ended in death. Even Malcolm did not know how absolute was the laird's need, not simply of air and freedom, but of all things accompanying the enjoyment of them.

"There was nothing, then, of insanity in his preference of a windowless bedroom; it was that airs and odours, birds and sunlight — the sound of flapping wing, of breaking wave, and quivering throat — might be free to enter. Cool, clean air he must breathe, or die; with that, the partial confinement to which he was subjected was not unendurable. . . .

"He not only loved but understood all the creatures, divining by an operation in which neither the sympathy nor the watchfulness was the less perfect that both were but half conscious, the emotions and desires informing their inarticulate language. Many of them seemed to know him in return — either recognizing his person, and from experience deducing safety, or reading his countenance sufficiently to perceive that his interest prognosticated no injury. The maternal bird would keep her seat in her nursery, and give back his gaze; the rabbit peeping from his burrow would not even draw in his head at his approach. . . .

"He could make a bird's nest, of any sort common in the neighbourhood, so as to deceive the most cunning of the nest-harrying youths of the parish.

"Hardly was he an hour in his new abode ere the sparrows and robins began to visit him. Even strange birds of passage flying in at his hospitable window, would espy him unscared, and sometimes partake of the food he had always at hand to offer them. He relied indeed, for the pleasures of social intercourse with the animal world, on stray visits alone; he had no pets — dog nor cat nor bird; for his wandering and danger-haunted life did not allow such companionship."

There is evidently in the mind of the author an intelligent preference for the open-air treatment of patients suffering from mental or bodily disease.

There are several references in the end of the story to the epileptic seizures from which the poor laird suffered. He was frightened, and left his garret, wandered away, and at last wandered back to his unkind mother. The end of his poor troubled life comes soon after. He suffers from a terrible convulsion, but regains consciousness before he dies, and smiles, apparently seeing a beautiful vision just before the end comes.

Spinal tuberculosis was probably little understood when the book was written, and the author can hardly be expected to distinguish clearly the three distinct conditions of idiocy, insanity, and epilepsy. Yet there is a good deal of truth in the picture given. It is well known that mental deterioration occurs in many epileptics; and it is natural and right for us all, mentally strong and weak alike, to crave as much freedom and open air as we can have, consistent with the safety and comfort of ourselves and others.

Farm colony life for mentally defective persons is intended to give them the maximum of freedom and development.

Sir Gibbie

This story is a wonderful study of a boy who was supposed by some to be mentally defective, but was really both singularly gifted and attractive. In chapter XI we read of his "bewitching smiles," and in the first words of the story we learn of his care and protection of his father, a chronic alcoholic, — a care that was not only long-lasting but wise and ingenious and more purposeful than is possible with the mentally defective. Altogether the impression Sir Gibbie makes on the mind of the reader is the impression made by a normal character, though the poor fellow is unable to speak probably because he was deaf and there was no one to teach him lip-reading and speech. The power of speech would have changed the whole life of Sir Gibbie, loving, innocent, gifted — and yet outside the pale, and sadly misunderstood, because he cannot speak. Yet the reader has the confident feeling that Sir Gibbie's mind is all right, so that it comes as a shock when near the middle of the book the brutal gamekeeper, Angus MacPholp, calls Sir Gibbie an idiot in the soliloquy he holds with himself as he lies on the floor of Robert Grant's cottage, bound hand and foot for his misdeeds.

The story goes on to unfold a character of uncommon sagacity and sweetness. Sir Gibbie begins to pick out tunes on his "Pan's pipes" and discovers that he can produce tones, delighted too to find that the noises he makes are recognized by others as song, especially by Ginevra, the heroine of the tale, who hears the sound of his pipes, and is rescued by the "Beast-Boy," as the country folk call him, when she is lost on the mountain. The narrative reaches, perhaps, its highest point in the account of the great floods, and the remarkable rescue by Sir Gibbie not only of Ginevra, but (a far more ingenious and difficult rescue) of his brutal tormentor, Angus MacPholp. Any possible doubts which the reader might have had as to the mental powers of the hero vanish, when he exhibits a strength of will and initiative rare indeed, and, with no one to assist him, but with the powers of nature and human nature against him, rescues "A friend, a foe and a beast of the earth." For the remarkable and at the same time almost incredible incidents of the flood, the author has availed himself of Sir Thomas Dick Lauder's account of the historical Morayshire floods in 1829.

There is never a Scotch story without a clergyman, and in chapter xxxvii the Reverend Clement Sclater, who had made some inquiries as to the kin of Sir Gibbie's mother and found them wealthy and hard-hearted, sets down his breakfast cup of coffee untasted and rushes from the room to take action when he reads in the morning paper of the sudden death, intestate, of Sir Gibbie's uncle, leaving an estate of two hundred thousand pounds. However, before the calamity of riches overtakes Sir Gibbie, he has a few days among the mountains with the heroine, in conditions which occur in novels but not often elsewhere. She finds him the gentlest, kindest, and most interesting of companions. In daring, swiftness, and certainty when diving, swimming, and climbing, he rivals the bird of the air and the fish of the sea. He is able also to explain to her the marvels of mountain, sky, and water. This is a great contrast to the poor motor and muscular powers, the lack of coördination and the inapt and ungraceful movements of the mental defective, who possesses neither the powers of the body nor the treasures of the mind which made Sir Gibbie so delightful and interesting a companion.

The Reverend Mr. Sclater now appears on

the scene and captures Gibbie for the great
world, which Gibbie finds not so much to his
liking as the mountain and the moor. Yet his
smiles made a way for him. "Unhappily for
me there is no way of giving the delicate differences of those smiles. Much of what Gibbie
perhaps felt the more that he could not say it,
had got into the place where the smiles were
made, and, like a variety of pollens, had impregnated them with all shades and colours
of expression, whose varied significance those
who had known him longest, dividing and distinguishing, had gone far towards being able
to interpret. In that which now shone on Mrs.
Sclater, there was something, she said next
day to a friend, which no woman could resist,
and which must come of his gentle blood."
Such smiles are not seen in the mentally defective, though to those who take an interest
in them and are well inclined towards them,
the smile which comes to answer kindness and
help has an attraction and an appeal of its own.

Another incident accompanying Sir Gibbie's
plunge into this new world shows at once a
lack of self-regard and care for clothes, a sen-
sitive consciousness of bodily discomfort, and

an originality and vigor of resolution to which
mental defectives are strangers:

"Gibbie could endure cold or wet or hunger,
and sing like a mavis; he had borne pain upon
occasion with at least complete submission;
but the tight arm-holes of his jacket could
hardly be such a degree of Providence as it was
rebellion to interfere with; and therefore I do
not relate what follows, as a pure outcome of
that benevolence in him which was yet equal
to the sacrifice of the best-fitting of garments.
As they walked along Pearl Street, the hand-
somest street of the city, he darted suddenly
from Mrs. Sclater's side, and crossed to the
opposite pavement. She stood and looked after
him wondering, hitherto he had broken out in
no vagaries! As he ran, worse and worse! he
began tugging at his jacket, and had just succeeded in getting it off as he arrived at the
other side, in time to stop a lad of about his
own size, who was walking barefooted and
in his shirt-sleeves — if *shirt* or *sleeves* be a
term applicable to anything visible upon him.
With something of the air of the tailor who had
just been waiting upon himself, but with as
much kindness and attention as if the boy had

been Donal Grant instead of a stranger, he
held the jacket for him to put on. The lad
lost no time in obeying, gave him one look and
nod of gratitude, and ran down a flight of steps
to a street below, never doubting his benefactor
an idiot, and dreading some one to whom he
belonged would be after him presently to
reclaim the gift. Mrs. Sclater saw the proceed-
ing with some amusement and a little fore-
boding. She did not mourn the fate of the
jacket; had it been the one she had just
ordered, or anything like it, the loss would
have been to her not insignificant; but was the
boy altogether in his right mind? She in her
black satin on the opposite pavement, and the
lad scudding down the stair in the jacket, were
of similar mind concerning the boy, who, in
shirt-sleeves indubitable, now came bounding
back across the wide street. He took his place
by her side as if nothing had happened, only
that he went along swinging his arms as if he
had just been delivered from manacles. Having
for so many years roamed the streets with
scarcely any clothes at all, he had no idea of
looking peculiar, and thought nothing more of
the matter."

Then did Mr. Sclater teach him Latin and "the minister began to think it might be of advantage to learning in general, if at least half the boys and girls at school, and three parts of every Sunday congregation, were as dumb as Sir Gilbert Galbraith. When at length he set him to Greek, he was astonished at the avidity with which he learned it." This will help to convince the reader that Gibbie was not mentally defective, and the object of George MacDonald is now probably sufficiently attained to show how mistaken people may be in the judgment of the mental caliber of others. Yet the mental reactions of Gibbie in the realm of spiritual conduct are perhaps still more worth study: "Middling good people are shocked at the wickedness of the wicked; Gibbie, who knew both so well, and what ought to be expected, was shocked only at the wickedness of the righteous."

The romance of the story comes to a charming conclusion, as is the wont of the romances of George MacDonald, which always have a glory and sweetness of their own. But the rest of the life of Sir Gibbie, and of how clever he was in mathematics (diagnostic of *not* being feeble-minded, again!) and of the woman who loved him, must be read in the chronicles of George MacDonald.

George Eliot — Brother Jacob

In "Brother Jacob," one of her short stories, George Eliot tells the disagreeable tale of David Faux who is a Uriah Heep sort of person, despicable alike in body and soul. He has an ambition to travel and, being employed by a confectioner, takes from his master's till the money he wants for this purpose. It is not enough, so he steals some more from his own mother and buries his ill-gotten gains in the earth. Brother Jacob, the idiot, sees him doing this on a Sunday afternoon, "the third Sunday in Lent." After much trouble, David pacifies Jacob, and finally puts his plan of running away to travel into execution. Six years after, he comes back under the assumed name of Edward Freely and is just on the eve of making his way and arranging a marriage with Miss Penelope Palfrey when his plans are spoiled by Brother Jacob's recognizing him. It is "an admirable instance of the unexpected forms in which the great Nemesis hides herself."

This story is remarkable for the accurate knowledge displayed by the author. George Eliot understood the situation when she said, "David, not having studied the psychology of idiots, was not aware that they are not to be wrought upon by imaginative fears."

Joseph Conrad — The Idiots

A short story of Joseph Conrad's called "The Idiots" occurs in a volume of short stories under the general title of "Tales of Unrest." It is a French tale in which a man and his wife, apparently normal, meet the almost incredible tragedy of finding that all their children are idiotic. The anguish of the situation is powerfully depicted, but it will at once occur to any intelligent person to doubt if two normal persons, such as the man and his wife presumably are, could have idiotic children only. No such case seems to be recorded. It is a tale of unrest. Let no one be disturbed by it.

Robert Louis Stevenson — Olalla

A volume of short stories by Robert Louis Stevenson called "The Merry Men" contains

a tale called "Olalla." The scene is laid in
Spain and the narrator is a wounded officer
whose doctor has sent him to the house of some
Spanish grandees to complete his convales-
cence. The boy Felipe, who drives him to the
castle of the grandees, seems to be an imbecile.
He shows marked cruelty to a squirrel, and
displays other marks of mental defect, but he
possesses marvelous agility, which is not usual
in an imbecile. Some one in the castle is apparently subject to attacks of insanity. The
officer at last sees Olalla, falls hopelessly in
love with her, but finally yields to her en-
treaties that he should leave the place at once,
and forever.

THE WRECKER

Robert Louis Stevenson draws the picture of
Tommy Hadden, a high-grade mental defective, in "The Wrecker." When Mr. Carthew,
the "Remittance Man," comes back to Sydney
after doing "Homeric labour in Homeric circumstance," Tommy recognizes him and
hails him in a loud voice, and Mr. Carthew,
"turning about, found himself face to face
with a handsome sunburnt youth, somewhat

fatted, arrayed in the finest of fine raiment, and sporting about a sovereign's worth of flowers in his buttonhole. . . .

"Tom Hadden (known to the bulk of Sydney folk as Tommy) was heir to a considerable property, which a prophetic father had placed in the hands of rigorous trustees. The income supported Mr. Hadden in splendour for about three months out of twelve; the rest of the year he passed in retreat among the islands. He was now about a week returned from his eclipse, pervading Sydney in hansom cabs and airing the first bloom of six new suits of clothes; . . ."

At the moment, Tommy is engrossed in a grand scheme for island trade. He and Mr. Carthew go to consult Captain Bostock, who knows all that is to be known on that subject.

"Doubtless the Captain was a mine of counsel, but opportunity was denied him. He could not venture on a statement, he was scarce allowed to finish a phrase, before Hadden swept him from the field with a volley of protest and correction."

"You know a sight, don't you?" remarked

that gentleman, bitterly, when Tommy paused.

"I know a sight more than you, if that's what you mean," retorted Tom. "It stands to reason I do. You're not a man of any education; you've been all your life at sea or in the islands; you don't suppose you can give points to a man like me?"

"Here's your health, Tommy," returned Bostock. "You'll make an A-1 bake in the New Hebrides."

"That's what I call talking," cried Tom, not perhaps grasping the spirit of this doubtful compliment. "Now you give me your attention. We have the money and the enterprise, and I have the experience; what we want is a cheap, smart boat, a good Captain and an introduction to some house that will give us credit for the trade."

"Well, I'll tell you," said Captain Bostock. "I seen men like you baked and eaten, and complained of afterwards. Some was tough, and some had n't no flaviour," he added grimly.

"What do you mean by that?" cried Tom.

"I mean I don't care," said Bostock. "It

ain't any of my interests. I have n't underwrote
your life. Only I'm blest if I'm not sorry for
the cannibal as tries to eat your head. And
what I recommend is a cheap, smart coffin and
a good undertaker. See if you can find a house
to give you credit for a coffin! Look at your
friend there; *he's* got some sense; he's laughing at you so as he can't stand."

Drawn to the life. The voluble high-grade
mental defective, "wiser than seven men who
can render a reason," is an exasperating being.
Sometimes he or she would almost deceive
the very elect. Is it any wonder they impose
on many persons, including even some magistrates and judges?

Mrs. Robert Louis Stevenson, in her recently published book, "The Cruise of the
Janet Nichol," gives some additional particu-
lars about "Tommy Hadden." His real name
was John, not Tom, and he was known on
board the "Janet Nichol" as "Tin Jack,"
"Tin" being the South Sea equivalent for
"Mister."

Tin Jack goes on the cruise armed with a
false face, an enormous false nose, and other
disguises, which he used to great effect to

frighten the natives. He forgets things very often, and on one occasion he forgets about Mrs. Stevenson's return to the ship, and she is left in a sad plight for two or three hours because of this.

Mrs. Stevenson thus finishes the tale of his life.

"Tin Jack came to a sad end. He possessed a certain fixed income, which, however, was not large enough for his ideas, so he spent most of the year as a South Sea trader, using the whole of his year's income in one wild burst of dissipation in the town of Sydney. One of his favourite amusements was to hire a hanson cab for a day, put the driver inside, and drive the vehicle himself, calling upon various passers-by to join him at the nearest public-house. In the end when Jack was at his station he received word that his trustee, who was in charge of his property, had levanted with it all. Whereupon poor Jack put a pistol to his head and blew out what brains he possessed. He was a beautiful creature, terribly annoying at times, but with something childlike and appealing — I think he was close to what the Scotch call a natural — that made one forgive pranks in him that would

be unforgivable in others. He was very proud
of being the original of Tommy Hadden in
the 'Wrecker,' and carried the book with him
wherever he went."

CHAPTER IV

NATHANIEL HAWTHORNE — THE MARBLE FAUN

NATHANIEL HAWTHORNE, in "The Marble Faun," uses his wonderful gifts of imagination to tell another story that should be read when one is quite young, as a maturer judgment somewhat spoils one's pleasure with too many doubts as to whether such a person as Donatello could ever have lived.

He (Donatello) is called "underwitted" by one of the other characters, and it is hinted that his ears are pointed, and that he is much like a marble faun himself. He seems to be represented as less than human and therefore different from a mental defective, who is human.

"How old should you think him, Hilda?"

"Twenty years, perhaps," replied Hilda, glancing at Donatello; "but, indeed, I cannot tell; hardly so old, on second thoughts, or possibly older. He has nothing to do with time, but has a look of eternal youth in his face."

"All underwitted people have that look," said Miriam scornfully.

The beautiful Hilda, beloved of the American artist, herself an American girl; Miriam, the beautiful Jewess, whose character is mysterious and incomprehensible, with a shadow of crime behind it, and Donatello, for whom Miriam has an overwhelming attraction, are the chief characters in the story.

It is more than once hinted that Donatello's ancient family had once owned an ancestor who was not altogether human.

The unhappy occurrence in the Catacomb, by which Miriam meets some person who haunts her like a specter and interrupts both her pleasures and her work, is the shadow of that coming event which is the tragedy of the story.

"One of Miriam's friends took the matter sadly to heart. This was the young Italian. Donatello, as we have seen, had been an eyewitness of the stranger's first appearance, and had ever since nourished a singular prejudice against the mysterious, dusky, death-scented apparition. It resembled not so much a human dislike or hatred, as one of those instinctive, unreasoning antipathies which the lower animals sometimes display, and which generally prove more trustworthy than the acutest insight into character. The shadow of the model, always flung into the light which Miriam diffused around her, caused no slight trouble to Donatello. Yet he was of a nature so remarkably genial and joyous, so simply happy, that he might well afford to have something subtracted from his comfort, and make tolerable shift to live upon what remained."

In the end, when Miriam and Donatello are left alone, the "specter" appeared. Donatello is so angry at seeing the unhappiness of Miriam, that he is the means of the death of the "specter" by dashing him over a cliff.

After this occurrence Donatello is never happy again. We have a glimpse of him as host to Kenyon at his own castle of Beni, but the terrible secret haunts him, and the woman whom he loves, and makes him a different person. Kenyon thinks that "From some mysterious source, as the sculptor felt assured, a soul had been inspired into the young Count's simplicity, since their intercourse in Rome. He now showed a far deeper sense, and an intelligence that began to deal with high subjects, though in a feeble and childish way. He evinced, too, a more definite and nobler individuality, but developed out of grief and pain, and fearfully conscious of the pangs that had given it birth. Every human life, if it ascends to truth or delves down to reality, must undergo a similar change; but sometimes, perhaps, the instruction comes without the sorrow; and oftener the sorrow teaches no lesson that abides with us. In Donatello's case, it was pitiful, and almost ludicrous, to observe the confused struggle that he made; how completely he was taken by surprise; how ill-prepared he stood, on this old battle-field of the world, to fight with such an inevitable foe as mortal calamity, and sin for its stronger ally."

In the end it is hinted that Donatello is imprisoned for his crime; and the last glimpse of Miriam, who is supposed to have influential connections in Rome, and perhaps to have something to do with political intrigues, is as a penitent, kneeling.

This fanciful story while it does not add another to the mentally defective characters in literature, is interesting as an indication of people's ideas on this subject.

ALICE HEGAN RICE — MR. OPP

Alice Hegan Rice, in "Mr. Opp," tells the story of a mentally defective girl "Kippy." The writer, however, speaks of her as "half-crazed," not distinguishing the two conditions.

Mr. D. Webster Opp, who is Kippy's brother, appears at the opening of the story, attending his stepfather's funeral.

"You don't," says Mr. Opp to his brother Ben, "know Kippy; she's just similar to a little child, quiet and gentle-like. Never give anybody any trouble in her life. Just plays with her dolls, and sings to herself all day."

"Exactly," said Ben; "twenty-five years old and still playing with dolls. I saw her yesterday dressed up in all sorts of foolish toggery, talking to her hands, and laughing. Aunt Tish humors her, and her father humored her, but I'm not going to. I feel sorry for her all right, but I am not going to take her home with me."

"D. Webster nervously twisted the large seal ring which he wore on his forefinger.

"Then what do you mean," he said hesitatingly — "what do you want to do about it?"

"Why, send her to an asylum, of course. That's where she ought to have been all these years."

"Send Kippy to a lunatic asylum!" he said in tones so indignant that they made his chin tremble. "You will do nothing whatever of the kind! Why, all she's ever had in the world was her pa and Aunt Tish and her home; now he's gone, you ain't wanting to take the others away from her too, are you?"

So Kippy remains with her brother, Mr. D. Webster Opp.

The crisis in the story is reached when Mr. Opp falls in love with Guinevere Gusty and Kippy finds and reads a letter written by Guinevere containing these words, "Mother says I can never marry you till Kippy goes to the asylum." Poor Kippy then runs away from home to the asylum where her brother finally discovers her and brings her home.

Mr. Opp's peculiarities are made much of

in the story, but the writer shows her kindness of heart in giving him a position in the respect and esteem of his fellow citizens. While he was making a speech at the banquet tendered to him on the occasion of his retirement from his newspaper "The Opp Eagle," Aunt Tish arrives with a message that the poor feeble-minded girl needs him —

"Hit's Miss Kippy," she whispered. "I hate to 'sturb you, but she done crack her doll's head, an' she's takin' on so I can't do nuffin't all wif her."

"Could n't you contrive to get her quiet no way at all?" asked Mr. Opp anxiously.

"Naw, sir. She mek like dat doll her shore 'nough baby, and she 'low she gwine die, too, furst chanct she gits. I got Val's mother to stay wif her till I git back."

"All right," said Mr. Opp hastily. "You go right on and tell her I'm coming."

"When he reëntered the dining-room he held his hat in his hand.

"I find an urgent matter of business calls me back home; for only a few moments I trust," he said apologetically, with bows and smiles. "If the banquet will kindly proceed, I will endeavor to return in ample time for the final speeches."

"With the air of a monarch taking temporary leave of his subjects, he turned his back upon the gay, protesting crowd, upon the feast prepared in his honor, upon the speech-making so dear to his heart. Tramping through the snow of the deserted street, through the lonely graveyard, and along the river road, he went to bind up the head of a china doll, and to wipe away the tears of a little half-crazed sister.

"He wears the same checked suit as when we saw him first, worn and frayed, to be sure, but carefully pressed for the occasion, the same brave scarf and pin, and watch fob, though the watch is missing.

Passing out of sight with the sleet in his face, and the wind cutting through his finery, he whistles as he goes, such a plucky, sturdy, hopeful whistle as calls to arms the courage that lies slumbering in the hearts of men."

There is a still kinder way of caring for mental defectives. A way that is wiser and more just, as well as kinder.

KATE DOUGLAS WIGGIN — MARM LISA

Alisa Bennett, a girl of about ten or twelve years of age when the story opens, is represented as feeble-minded and apparently epileptic. She is living with a Mrs. Grubb, who is described as "not a home spirit" and very fond of starting a society or association for every possible thing. She takes no care of her children, who are frequently referred to as "Atlantic" and "Pacific." They are troublesome children and need a good deal of care, which is given to them partly by the husband of Mrs. Grubb but much more by Alisa.

Alisa and the children find their way to a free kindergarten. The rest of the story is an account of the way in which the poor feeble-minded girl worshiped Mistress Mary, who is the Principal of the Kindergarten, and what Mistress Mary and her assistants did for Alisa.

There are many passages in the book which can hardly be regarded either as reasonable or accurate. Apparently the author thinks it is possible to cure mental defect. She says, for example, "that the other children became aware that a human mind was tottering to its fall and that Mistress Mary was engaged in preventing it." She makes several allusions to alleged medical opinions, and she represents Mistress Mary, with the steel band she wore in her hair, as the possessor of more power than we poor mortals really have. However, the object of the book is in every way excellent and no doubt it has helped to waken interest in and compassion for the feeble-minded. The book reaches its climax in a fire and Marm Lisa shows herself a heroine in this fire, saving the lives of Atlantic and Pacific.

In spite of some passages which can hardly be regarded as anything but absurd, this book is interesting as recording one of the phases in the history of the recognition and treatment of the feeble-minded in the community.

S. P. McL. Greene — Vesty of the Basins

In "Vesty of the Basins," by Sarah P. McL. Greene, there appears a feeble-minded person, Uncle Benny, who was treated kindly by the other inhabitants of the Basins.

He meets Vesty and her lover.

"Here is a good sign; so the Basins held. No sign so propitious to a love affair as meeting with one of God's innocent ones — a 'natural.' And here was Dr. Spearmint (Uncle Benny) leading the children to school — the very little ones. They clung, and one he carried."

He makes himself useful by caring for the very little children on the way to school and back again; he loves bright colors; he repeats the same phrase again and again, and has a very limited number of ideas, characteristic of the class to which he belongs. He is very easily deceived, he has some knowledge of music, and is represented in the story as living alone. He is very affectionate — the greatest thing in the character of a mental defective, as it is in that of any other human being.

ARNOLD MULDER — BRAM OF THE FIVE CORNERS

Many books contain one character more or less mentally defective, but, except "Bram," "Marm Lisa," and "Barnaby Rudge," there are perhaps none where one of the leading characters is feeble-minded, and where the history and nature of mental defect is closely interwoven with the plot. Mental defect is the main theme of the story in "Bram." The scene is laid in rural Michigan, among the Dutch or Hollanders, who are represented as so ignorant, narrow-minded, and unprogressive that the reader wonders if the settlement described is a typical one, or if it is quite exceptional in respect to the character of the people living there. The skill of the author is rather that of the journalist than of the novelist, but the interest in the story is well sustained.

The book is a sign of the times and will be read with keen interest by those concerned about social problems. Perhaps the most attractive character in the book is the young minister, who was as progressive as his people were unprogressive and as much inclined to be kind as they were to be harsh.

When Bram, the hero of the story, was fourteen years old, he went "berry-picking" to the woods by the lake, along with all the other boys and girls of the Five Corners. It was "a rough-and-tumble, rapturous, care-free rural picnic." In the course of the afternoon he lost his way and his halloo was answered by a girl, also lost in the woods, named Hattie Wanhope, a pretty girl, who "giggled a great deal and . . . chattered incessantly."

The shy, timid country boy began to dream
and to be greatly attracted by the girl, who
was neither shy nor timid, and three years
older than the boy. Before many months their
attachment was noticed in the Five Corners
and one good lady demanded — "What is the
world comin' to, . . . boys and girls is hardly
out of their baby dresses but they start to
'go together.'"

Bram was a boy capable of great things, and
the young minister, who was the greatest
influence for good in Bram's early life, realized
this, and said to him one day — "I like to
think of you a few years hence as a man who
will not think of himself alone; nor yet only
of the woman you will marry; I like to think
of you as a man who will leave the race stronger
than you found it."

The death of the young minister leaves
Bram without a guide, but his eyes are gradu-
ally opened to the fact that Hattie, whom he
intended to marry, must be feeble-minded. He
hears a lecture upon "The Child Who Never
Grows Up," by Dr. Victor. Bram sees Dr.
Victor afterwards and hears from him that
"It can be predicted as definitely as anything

can be predicted that the man who marries a
feeble-minded woman or the woman who
marries a feeble-minded man will bring a curse
upon the children. And they contribute towards
retarding the development of a better and
stronger race of men. May I add that for such
a man to pray for the coming of the Kingdom
of God seems sacrilege to me."

As usual, Bram could have learned this
without going to Dr. Victor. The farmers of
the Five Corners had no difficulty in making
a diagnosis of the Wanhope family. "To the
boys of the Five Corners the family did not
seem entirely 'impossible'; to them Hattie was
the Wanhope family. But the men and women
of the community did not allow their judg-
ments to be warped by a pretty face. To them
the Wanhope family seemed an alien element.

"Nor did the prettiness of Hattie warp the
judgment of the very small boys of the Five
Corners. 'Crazy Chris' was the name they had
invented for the head of the house, and un-
consciously their elders adopted the term.

"The barn of Chris Wanhope was the
scandal of the Five Corners. There was not
another barn like it within a radius of five

miles; that is to say, there was not another barn like it as far as the horizon of the people of the community extended. No farmer of the Five Corners could ever repress a feeling of resentment when he passed the Wanhope farm and saw the old patchwork of rough boards and shingles that housed the cattle and in which the hay and grain were stored."

"Why, it ain't no barn," Berend would say to Anton; "it's nothin' more than a shed, and a mighty poor shed at that."

"His cows look it," Anton would answer; "their hair's grown twice as long as that of other cows. They're like bears in the far North what grow hair in winter to protect them against the cold. Them cows of Chris have got to keep warm somehow, and that's the only way — what with cracks in the barn a foot wide."

"Have you been inside?"

"Once." Chris Wanhope was not one of the people of the Five Corners although he lived among them. They did not visit him in his barn, as they visited frequently in the barns of other neighbors.

"But no matter what improvements Chris's neighbors made, the barn of Chris Wanhope remained a 'shed.' When all the others erected silos Chris continued to store his corn stalks in the primitive way, and all the other improvements that followed left him where he had always been. It was absolutely unthinkable that he should ever make any repairs that the wind and the rain and the frost did not compel him to make; and even then they were made only after some mischief had been done to the stock.

"The good opinion of his neighbors never meant anything to him. He did not realize that he was not living up to the social standards of the community.

"It was well known to the people of the Five Corners, and it was often told by them to visitors, that Chris never had been known to split his kindling wood in the evening; he invariably waited until he needed it in the morning. Then he shuffled through the snow, found a board or a 'chunk,' frequently ripping the board off a fence, if no other fuel was at hand, and split the kindling for the morning's fire. When he reasoned about it at all his logic was to the effect that the fence would not be needed again until the following summer and that it was no use worrying so long ahead. The fire, however, was needed at that moment."

After his long talk with Dr. Victor, Bram of course feels that he must not marry Hattie and he tries to tell her so. "But she did not understand. And it came to Bram all at once that she could never be made to understand. . . . A quart measure can never be educated to hold a bushel."

The Church and the community turn against Bram, and he has to leave the Five Corners and go to the city. After a good many difficulties he finds employment on "The Sun" as a reporter. He gains the confidence of the editor, Mr. Craik, who tells him one night — "It is n't the calling I lay stress on; it's the spirit in which the work is done."

"What is the Gospel of 'The Sun'?" Mr. Craik continued. "Is n't it the wide human charity that Jesus Christ himself preached? When the red-light district was driven out last year, did n't 'The Sun' call attention to the fact that the women deprived of a livelihood were women with souls and that merely driving them out did not end the task? The good people were throwing stones. I am not blaming them. They were sincere for the most part. They merely did not think. They did not realize that throwing stones is not all that is necessary. Christ treated the woman of the red-light district as a sister. And 'The Sun' preached to sixty thousand people the gospel of doing the same. It was done imperfectly, I admit. Yet the sincere impulse was there to hold this course up as a not impossible ideal. 'The Sun,' or any other paper for that matter, is not regenerating society in a generation. I used to think it would but I have learned to readjust my ideas. There is nearly as much selfishness and uncharitableness here as there was seventeen years ago when I began my work; but not *quite* as much. I believe there is a narrow margin of advance. And that narrow margin gives me enthusiasm for going on. Neither for that matter does the minister in the pulpit regenerate even his small flock in a generation.''

Bram makes his way, and finds happiness. He does not forget poor Hattie, whom he attempts to befriend more than once, always with no success. Hers is the sad fate of the pretty, feeble-minded girl. This story gives a true picture of the problem of caring for mentally defective persons in our modern communities.

The Contributors' Club

In January, 1917, the following remarkable contribution appeared in the ".Atlantic Monthly."

The visitors in the Court represent Public Opinion. People are beginning to feel that "Something will have to be done" about the feeble-minded and that we must do it.

Heritages of the Lord

The sun shone through the high windows on the judge's yellow hair. It touched the calf-skin volumes on his orderly desk. It glowed through the folds of the large silk flag above the bookcase. Yes, the court-room was tolerable. But not the sun itself could brighten the sordid room across the hall, — that room packed with grimy, lowering fathers, grimy, worried mothers, grimy, sullen, abnormal children.

"Next case," said the judge curtly.

A starchy probation officer laid papers before him. She looked like an animated ledger. She, if any one, could convince you that we are made of carbohydrates and proteids, and that the joy of life is a mere figure of speech.

The ushers fluttered about a grimy caravan that came in from across the hall. They ranged their charges before the court. In front were a small boy and girl. Their clothes seemed impregnated with the dust of ages. The little girl's dress alone would have sufficed to silt up the multitudinous seas.

"Your Honor, Mr. Housel asks the court to commit these children to homes," said the probation officer.

The judge fumbled the papers. He turned calm, blue eyes on the father.

"I committed two of Mr. Housel's children last year," he remarked.

The man's hat, once black, was now green. He turned it round in his stiff fingers. With a face all anxious goodness, he watched the judge.

"The mother can't keep them from running the streets," stated the probation officer. "She's feeble-minded. She has no control over them."

The grimy woman plucked at her husband's sleeve, and muttered unintelligibly.

"How about the father?" asked the judge.

Shuffling his lumpy boots, the man cast his eyes on the judge's blue silk socks and patent leather shoes.

"*He's* all right," the probation officer replied. "Sober, kind, hard-working. He makes two dollars a day regularly."

"Why can't he control the children?"

"He's away all day, your Honor. He works on the railroad."

"Can't the mother be advised? Is there no hope of improved conditions?"

"No, your Honor. She's feeble-minded."

The judge frowned at his neat finger-nails. He addressed the father, mildly.

"Where does your wife come from?"

The grimy man lifted his gaze from the blue silk socks to the blue eyes.

"From Virginia, Judge," he stammered.

"You married her in Virginia?"

"Yes, Judge."

"How old was she?"

"Seventeen."

Evidently this draggled creature, who looked

as if she had been salvaged from an ash-barrel, was actually seventeen, once upon a time.

"Virginia allows feeble-minded persons to marry," commented the probation officer.

The probation officer was clean and practical. Life showed her only its black and white. No dusty section-hand had ever courted her in Virginia in May. And yet perhaps even probation officers are marriageable at seventeen. Now, with unemotional ease, she discussed the feeble mind of the grimy woman in the grimy woman's presence.

"You wish me to commit' these children as I did the others last year?" the judge turned to the father.

"Yes, judge."

The woman plucked again at her husband's sleeve, inarticulate.

"She wants to keep the baby," he ventured to the probation officer. He dared not address this bold demand to the court.

"Which is the baby?" inquired the judge.

"The baby is n't here," explained the probation officer. "It's a little baby. Only a few months old. Born since you committed the others, last year."

"What do *you* think?" the judge asked the probation officer.

"Oh, she might as well keep the baby," she conceded, indifferently. "She can't do it any harm, yet."

The grimy woman's face relaxed its tension.

The judge signed commitment papers. The hearing was over.

"Next case," commanded the court as the grimy family filed out.

"But you can't let her keep the baby when it gets older," protested the visitors to the probation officer.

She shrugged.

"By that time there'll be another baby," she predicted.

"For the state to support!"

"For the state to support. Exactly."

"And the mother feeble-minded!" The visitors were horrified.

"They're all subnormal," added the probation officer.

And, remembering great families that have died out in Virginia, the visitors asked, "What of a state that lets its best stock perish, and permits a feeble-minded woman to bear five children?"

"Don't blame Virginia," remonstrated the probation officer. "She just happened to be from Virginia. Plenty of other states do the same thing. They won't restrict the liberty of the citizen."

The visitors exclaimed indignantly.

"Laws are much occupied with the rights of citizens. The right to be born, especially. Why should the law overlook the right of the citizen not to be born feeble-minded?"

Nobody seemed to know the answer.

"You say the father of those children works hard?" continued the visitors.

"He earns good wages," agreed the probation officer.

"Should n't the law have protected him and his descendants from this blight? If he had known that his children would be defective, can any one suppose he would have married such a woman? How could he know that she was feeble-minded? And he had a right to know."

The probation officer smiled commiseratingly. She was not paid to worry about the law.

CHAPTER V

GREAT writers have recognized the feeble-minded. They know that there are such people. When they painted the great world there was a place found on the canvas for the feeble-minded. Great writers discovered long before the modern "uplifter" was born that we must reckon with the mental defective as one of those many things in heaven and earth that are not dealt with by some philosophers, and yet that make a great difference to the community and to social progress.

Kindness is the key that unlocks the problem of the feeble-minded — kindness and wisdom. The feeble-minded must have a permanent guide, philosopher and friend, so Wamba has Cedric and Gurth, Maggy has Little Dorrit, Billy has Dr. Amboyne, and Henry Little, and Barnaby Rudge has his mother. Mental defectives cannot manage by themselves, though we have tried to pretend to the contrary.

As to our attitude towards them: Nicholas Nickleby "treated Smike like a human creature." So he was. So was the Fool in "Lear." So with the rest. They are human creatures — human beings, and differ among themselves in reactions, in character, in endowment, in emotion, almost as much as the rest of us. Yet while this is true, there remains a world of difference even in fiction between the normal and the mentally defective. Little Dorrit and Maggy, Gurth and Wamba, Gabriel Varden and Barnaby Rudge — the verdict is never in doubt for a moment. The one makes upon the reader the definite impression of a normal person, but the other is "not all there."

Give them a Chance

The Golden Rule applies to them. We are to do for them what we would others should do for us. Give them justice and a fair chance. Do not throw them into a world where the scales are weighted against them. Do not ask them to gather grapes of thorns or figs of thistles. But give them one chance to bring out the best that is in them. This is but a fair request on behalf of human beings who nevertheless are permanent children and who will never grow up — whose joys, and sorrows, and sins, and virtues are all on a childish scale. Responsibility, except so far as a child understands it, is not their portion. The achievements of life, for them, are bounded by their mental make-up and character — just as our own achievements are, though on a little larger scale.

So with their education. What was the use of teaching Toots to read and write? His letter-writing was a joke and did him more harm than good. His view of himself as to clothes and otherwise is that of a boy of about half his age.

Why condemn poor Smike to the agony of trying to do school tasks? They were beyond him, hopelessly and entirely beyond him. How cruel to expect him to learn, even at the age of nineteen, tasks which "a child of nine years old could have conquered with ease." Yet this suffering, this cruelty is commonly perpetrated in our schools. The unhappy mentally defective pupils are expected to learn what they cannot learn — urged, talked to and at — often held up to ridicule — when it is

not they, but we ourselves who are in fault.
Teach them what they *can learn* — not what
they *cannot learn*. That seems axiomatic, but
it is not yet accepted as an axiom. For they
can all learn something. Silly Billy "can beat
the town at one or two things." He learned
wood-carving and so was able to do his share
in the partnership. He could tell by the sound
when a stone turning in the works had a flaw
in it — that is, he was an expert — in stones.
So was Davie Gellatley — in roasting eggs.
So are all mental defectives — if we can only
find out their *métier*.

What we ought to do is to find out, in the
case of the feeble-minded in our own community, what their special gifts are. They have
gifts. But it takes a wise person to see the
strong points, the cleverness, the capacity,
of another. Any fool can find fault. Any passer-
by can show you a weak point. But the divin-
ing-rod does not work in every man's hand.
It was Jonathan who saw that David was to
be king in Israel. It was Andrew who went
and first found his own brother Simon. It was
Columbus who discovered America. It was
Lister who saw the meaning of Pasteur's dis-

coveries. It is the age of true democracy that
will not only give every one justice, but will
redeem the waste products of humanity and
give the mental defective all the chance he
needs to develop his gifts and all the protection he needs to keep away from him evils and
temptations that he never will be grown-up
enough to resist, and that society cannot
afford to let him fall a victim to. So developed
and encouraged the feeble-minded can almost
or quite maintain themselves, under care and
supervision, and that means, as a rule, residence in an institution. Even Squeers said of
Smike, "A handy fellow out of doors and
worth his meat and drink anyway."

Here is the darker side of the picture. How
many mental defectives like Smike and Guster
and Maggy are exploited and imposed on and
cruelly treated and robbed by the unscrupu-
lous? How many are deceived and persuaded
into criminal acts — even to murder, like
Barnaby Rudge, and so are cast into prison
and meet the punishment of felons? Yet they
have no real conception of what they are doing at all. The crimes of the anti-social are as
much a sealed book to them as the responsi-

bilities of the citizen. The same Barnaby Rudge, if left to his mother's influence, was happy, dutiful, harmless and able to help his mother to earn a living. Well did Hugh say of him that he "can be got to do anything if you take him the right way."

EASY TO MAKE HAPPY, SAFE, AND USEFUL

Simple pleasures and occupations are all the feeble-minded need. The occupations of children make them perfectly happy. Barnaby, a strong man, playing with his skein of string, listening to the same interminable story which his mother told him every day, and which he never remembered the next day, is the very type of the feeble-minded person who can be made and kept happy, safe and well occupied at little expense and with great success and benefit to himself and others. The marvelous improvement that care, kindness, and training bring about in the feeble-minded is almost incredible to those who have not learned it at first hand. Maggy, who "was never to be more than ten years old, however long she lived," under the motherly care of Little Dorrit "began to take pains to improve herself," "got enough to do to support herself," "was allowed to come in and out as often as she liked."

There are those like "Jo" and "Sloppy" and "Alice" who are accused of being mentally defective when they are far otherwise. Beware the gifted amateur, particularly those bearing Binet tests which they do not understand. Beware also the de-humanized expert — another great public danger. We should all consider ourselves "Counsel for the Accused" and never whisper "feeble-minded" unless and until mental defect is clearly and unquestionably proved.

The dark tragedies involved in this problem are, naturally, and properly enough, lightly touched upon in fiction. Miss Fanny, though she said Young Sparkler was "almost an idiot," and despised him for his mental feebleness, married him in the end. He could not earn a living — he had no more mind or will of his own than "a boat when it is towed by a steamship."

But we realize now, what no one realized then, that marriage with a mental defective brings the curse of mental defect upon the children. Many of the Susan Nippers and Miss

Fannys of the present generation know that now, and soon all will know it.

Little Dorrit showed right feeling and a true instinct in dealing with the mentally defective. She was a "Little Mother" to poor Maggy, but she said she would far rather see her sister working hard for a living than rich and married to Young Sparkler. We do wrong when we permit a mental defective to become a parent.

Those who know anything about the work of orphanages, refuges, and other charitable institutions, those who have been on duty in "locked wards" or maternity wards of hospitals, those who are aware of the problem of the poor unfathered baby (did you ever think to yourself how innocent that baby is!), those who work for prison reform — no such person needs to be told what feeble-mindedness costs in hard cash, in self-respect, in social degradation — and degeneracy. "Our duty to our neighbor must now be held to include our duty to posterity." We never shall conquer our two worst social evils until we deal with and remove this stumbling-block of the mental defective which stands in a causal relation to them both. It is not the only thing we have to do, but is there any other one thing that would help as much in solving our social problems as dealing firmly, wisely, and kindly with mentally defective persons?

These two problems are closely connected with each other, and they cannot be effectively dealt with unless we stop neglecting the mentally defective and reorganize charitable institutions, work for dependents and delinquents, procedure in criminal courts, and above all education and school-work, according to the facts, recognizing mental defectives as children, the wards of the state, who must receive the training, protection and care — in one word, the home that they need, so that they do not mingle with the general community. Hattie Wanhope was recognized at school. She should have been taken into care then. Poor Hattie is far more dangerous to the Nation than Maggy or Barnaby Rudge.

A hundred years ago people began to deal more justly, kindly, and sensibly with lunatics and with mental defectives, because they began to conjecture that lunatics were sick and had need of a physician and mental defectives were permanent children and needed permanent parents. In the hundred years since, in our well-meant efforts to do good, we have often only tried to help the mentally unfit to do the things they are unfit to do, such as attempting to make a home. The mentally defective are those who cannot make, or help to make, a home.

We must make a happy and permanent home for them during their lives. The only Permanent Parent is the State.

If a hundred years — and the Great War — and the sacrifice of the "chief of our strength" in this generation — the glory of our youth — who gave their lives for the Peace and the Freedom and the Justice of the world — if THIS — and the coming of Democracy, so that we all have a share in determining national thinking and acting — have made us wiser — and there are signs that seem to say "Yes" — then the mind of the Nation will rise nearer to the level of our great writers, and we shall see somewhat more clearly what is and what is not meant by this National problem of the mentally defective, and see our duty to them and to the Nation — and set ourselves to do it.